Todd – Congr[a]
your PEP 'journey
can be easy ?! [signature]
Oct '19

FIT TO LEAD

TRANSFORMING YOUR LEADERSHIP
WITH THE 5 PILLARS OF PERFORMANCE

MARCUS & SARI
MARSDEN

Candid Creation Publishing

First published May 2017
Reprinted October 2017, October 2018

Copyright © 2018 Marcus Marsden and Sari Marsden

All rights reserved. No part of this publication may be reproduced, stored in a retrieval system, or transmitted, in any form or by any means, electronic, mechanical, photocopying, recording or otherwise, without the prior permission of the publisher, except for inclusion of brief quotations in a review.

The information provided in this book is designed to provide helpful information on the subjects discussed. Consult a physician before performing any exercise programme, including the programmes in this book. It is your responsibility to evaluate your own medical and physical condition and to independently determine whether to perform, use or adapt any of the information or content provided in this book. Any exercise programme may result in injury. By voluntarily undertaking any exercise displayed in this book, you assume the risk of any resulting injury. The publisher and authors assume no responsibility or liability for any loss or damage suffered by any person as a result of the use or misuse of any of the information or content in this book.

Candid Creation Publishing books are available through most major bookstores in Singapore. For bulk order of our books at special quantity discounts, please email us at enquiry@candidcreation.com.

FIT TO LEAD
Transforming Your Leadership with the 5 Pillars of Performance

Author	: Marcus Marsden and Sari Marsden
Publisher	: Phoon Kok Hwa
Editor	: Ryan How
Layout	: Corrine Teng
Cover design	: Danijela Mijailovic
Published by	: Candid Creation Publishing LLP
	167 Jalan Bukit Merah
	#05-12 Connection One Tower 4
	Singapore 150167
Tel/Fax	: (65) 6273 7623
Website	: www.candidcreation.com
Facebook	: www.facebook.com/CandidCreationPublishing
Email	: enquiry@candidcreation.com
ISBN	: 978-981-11-3359-6 (paperback)/ 978-981-11-3545-3 (hardcover)

National Library Board, Singapore Cataloguing in Publication Data

Name(s): Marsden, Sari, 1979- | Marsden, Marcus, 1967- author.
Title: Fit to lead : transforming your leadership with the 5 pillars of performance / Sari & Marcus Marsden.
Description: Singapore : Candid Creation Publishing LLP, 2017.
Identifier(s): OCN 983822953 | ISBN 978-981-11-3545-3 (hardcover) | ISBN 978-981-11-3359-6 (paperback)
Subject(s): LCSH: Leadership. | Physical fitness. | Executives--Health and hygiene. | Self-actualization (Psychology)
Classification: DDC 658.4092--dc23

CONTENTS

CONCLUSION   Moving Forward

ACKNOWLEDGEMENTS

Writing a book in the field of personal development, coaching and leadership has been a daunting affair, because we are very aware that we are "standing on the shoulders of giants". We have both been fortunate to attract many powerful mentors and coaches who have supported us along the way. We offer our thanks to the following people:

FROM MARCUS AND SARI

To our clients who have generously allowed us to feature their stories as case studies in this book, your real-life examples bring everything to life and make the theoretical ideas accessible.

To Kelly Poulos, for your insane and contagious passion that has never wavered.

To Terrie Lupberger, Beatriz Garcia and Chris Balsley, for your gracious, gentle giving and for introducing us to the wisdom of the body.

To Ryan How and Phoon Kok Hwa, our long-suffering editor and publisher at Candid Creation, without whom this book would never have seen the light of day.

To book cover designer Danijela Mijailovic, book layout designer Corrine Teng, photographer Nigel Lau, and brand logo designer Zaki Ibrahim, for your creativity and understanding.

Thank you too to Liv Studio Singapore for allowing us to photograph in your studio.

FROM SARI

To Nike and the trainers of the Southeast Asian Nike+ Training Club team, for empowering me to become the best version of myself for the sake of others and for making sure I move dynamically by putting proper shoes on my feet.

To Tini Fadzillah, for bringing a light touch to our work in women's empowerment and leadership development.

To Jacqueline Lee, for guiding me with your knowledge of movement training. Your simple and sensible approach has been invaluable in helping me design the practices in this book.

To the students from Aidha and Mountbatten Vocational School, for welcoming me into your lives and constantly reminding me about the powerful mood of joy.

To Uci, Dini, Patsy, Indri, Lia, Ina, Sessa and Lisa, my precious circle of dynamic friends who never stop championing and challenging me in the process of growth. I am truly blessed to have you all in my life.

To my family, for loving me for who I am.

Finally to Marcus, there's a special sixth pillar of performance in my life, and that is you! I am especially thankful for the headphones.

FROM MARCUS

To Darren Rudkin and Bill McCabe, for believing in me when I took my early, faltering steps into this world of personal and leadership development. It was your early mentorship that really helped me believe I could actually flourish in this area.

To Mark Hemstedt, my long-time business partner at Newfield Asia and The Works Partnership, for letting me in to create a real partnership of equals in the company that you created.

To trainers Ken Ito and Doug Perasso, for challenging me to go far beyond the limits that I impose upon myself.

To my family: I think it is fair to say that you were all rather surprised when I upped and left marketing, Unilever and Europe in 2001. However, your unconditional love, support and encouragement have played a huge role in providing me with the secure foundation upon which my life and my work in this book is based.

Finally, to my wife and co-author, Sari, thank you for enduring all those early Oakland Raider mornings and late Bob Dylan nights.

FOREWORD

There are many books on leadership and many books on health, wellness and movement but few, if any, have made the direct link made here by Marcus and Sari. Most people still see leadership as a subject one learns or something one does that can be studied. As Marcus and Sari point out, we have pigeonholed leadership as a mental activity. The research however does not support this: in January 2015, *The Telegraph* summarised some of the research that shows statistical links between body weight and career progression.[1] Although there are certainly exceptions to every rule, anyone wishing to take on this thing called leadership should consider the body they walk around in. Although the research suggests that our body and health do play a part, research can only suggest a link. Research does not tell us what to do about it or how to make changes. That's where this book comes in.

I have had the pleasure of working with Marcus for over 15 years. I have known Sari for almost as long. Marcus always had a passion for learning and human behaviour. Sari has a passion for health and the body. They have always had a passion for each other that shows up in the joy they get from their work.

Marcus has always been a scholar of the work. He, like all great trainers and coaches in the personal development field, was willing to put on the white belt of a beginner and learn as an apprentice. As he practised over the years, he moved up the ranks from practitioner to virtuoso and is now an excellent trainer and coach. A master however is another step up the ladder. A master is one who takes the work and then makes it his or her own. This is what Marcus has done through his focus on leadership and fitness. Sari, not to be left behind, took it even further. As an international gold medal winner in the fitness industry, she is one of the leading talents in personal training and women's leadership in Asia. Together they make a formidable team.

---

1   www.telegraph.co.uk/men/thinking-man/11322225/Career-going-nowhere-Perhaps-its-because-youre-fat.html

This book is for anyone who wants to improve their leadership or their movement or both. It is for anyone who has the 21st century's most popular concern—work/life balance—or whatever that is. It is also for anyone who works in the coaching or fitness industries. After reading this book it is likely that you will no longer be able to separate the domains of fitness and work performance, or health and performance in any domain. Although medicine is helping us keep our bodies working for longer, it is still true that we really do only have one body and how we look after it determines our capacity to do anything and everything we want.

In some earlier work that Marcus and I were involved in, the comparison between a typical athlete and a typical executive was made. An athlete or sportsperson at the highest level spends most of their time preparing for that opportunity to perform at their best. To do this they work on everything. They eat well, hydrate well, sleep well, work on strength, speed, flexibility as well as the visualisation and mental side of their endeavour.

Then we take the typical executives that we meet in our line of work. They prepare themselves for peak performance by eating fast food, living on coffee, and express pride in the fact that they function on less sleep. If they exercise at all it is irregular and infrequent and seems to cause more injuries than sustained performance. Speed applies to everything except their physical being, and flexibility is seen as a weakness. The mental state is defined as keeping up with the latest management thinking or business news. Hobbies that used to build capacity have been sacrificed in the search for balance between life and work. After all this, executives expect themselves to deliver peak performance in that important meeting or that difficult discussion. Something here does not make sense, and Marcus and Sari are part of a leading group of people trying to change this.

At the end of this book you will likely be fitter or a better leader but if you take on their advice you might be both.

- Mark Hemstedt
Founding Partner, The Works Partnership

PREFACE

BY MARCUS

This book is the result of an ongoing journey, a journey that involves the clashing together of the many passions in my life: personal development, nutrition, leadership, sports, health and fitness, and coaching. Indeed, one of the central themes of this book is how the bringing together of seemingly disparate subjects and disciplines can illuminate new paths to the future. It is a journey that is still in progress.

I have been lucky. I have lived through one major change in leadership development and today, I believe that we are on the brink of another one. In fact, it is one that has been gathering pace for some time now and is about to become generally accepted.

The first major change occurred while I was working at Unilever. When I joined in 1989, Unilever had a well-deserved reputation for being one of the great developers of business talent in the world. However, after being in the company for a few years, I talked to HR managers and it was clear that they felt things needed updating. The company was still using techniques from the 1970s and 80s and while these techniques had once been cutting edge, they were now a little tired. The format was very didactic and lecture-based. It was really "school" for businessmen and businesswomen. The knowledge being imparted was still good, but it was not being retained. Not only that; with the pace of change picking up, the knowledge was also becoming less and less relevant.

There were two changes that really shook things up.

First of all, leadership development became far more experiential, an acknowledgement that human beings learn far more effectively by *doing* than by being talked at all day. Secondly, there was a realisation that leadership consisted of far more than what you know. Knowledge is all very well, but if you cannot *use* it effectively, it is largely a waste of time. A company is not a university. This was the time of Daniel Goleman and his groundbreaking book *Emotional Intelligence*, first published in 1995.

Gradually, this thinking began to infiltrate mainstream leadership development and it was in 2000 that I was fortunate to come across a company called The Works Partnership (TWP). Their work was highly experiential, very personal and focussed on "self-awareness" (Goleman lists self-awareness as the number one factor in developing emotional intelligence). This was a very different way of developing leaders. Suddenly, the focus was on *you*, the participant. *You* became the subject matter, not the case study, or the Powerpoint slide. In fact, there were no longer any case studies, Powerpoint slides, projectors or tables in the training room at all! Revolution!

Fast forward 20 years and we are on the cusp of another revolution. The big shift that happened after *Emotional Intelligence* was that, grudgingly, businesses had to acknowledge the existence and importance of emotions in leadership. The big shift we are experiencing now is that in addition to knowledge and emotion, the physical body is also beginning to be recognised as a critical element in leadership. This physical work has had its pioneers, just as the emotional work had Daniel Goleman. It appears to me that this work is on the cusp of breaking through and becoming accepted in mainstream leadership development in just the same way.

When emotions became an accepted part of leadership development, suddenly questions such as "How do you feel?" and "How do you think your manager feels when you do that?" went from being seen as weird to being seen as perfectly normal. When the physical body becomes similarly accepted as a key part of leadership development, questions such as "What did you eat yesterday?" and "When did you last exercise?" will also be seen as perfectly normal. We are not quite there yet, but it will not be long in coming.

For many years now I have been excited by the possibility of building connections between different disciplines and I have explored these ideas together with thousands of people in workshops, coaching sessions and simple conversations all over the world. I have also been fortunate to work and spend time with many wonderful teachers, mentors and co-conspirators over the years. What follows in this book is an attempt to synthesise many thousands of such conversations.

I am also more than fortunate to be on this journey with my wife and co-author Sari. She is the ideal companion for this journey: we agree on enough to be compatible, but not on so much as to be identical. You will see as much in her sections of the book. I hope you enjoy reading this book as much as we have enjoyed piecing it together.

BY SARI

This book is about a relationship. The relationship between Marcus and me, and the journey that we have been on together since the day we met. When I first met Marcus, I knew him as an executive coach and leadership trainer who was concerned with producing excellence through and with others. Over the next 10 years, I have watched him grow and develop into someone I now see as an athlete: someone who uses his body as well as his brain and his emotions in order to produce excellence.

In that same time, I have also developed and grown. What I find fascinating is that my journey and how Marcus sees me are almost the reverse of each other. My journey has seen me become an athlete in the more traditional sense of the word, as I now work as a personal trainer and with the Southeast Asian Nike+ Training Club (NTC) team. However, in that time, Marcus has come to see me not as an athlete but as a coach, a woman who makes it her job to support and challenge others to be excellent in their own lives.

As our lives and personal journeys have become intertwined through marriage, so our passions and interests have mingled and infused one another. This book is about our journey and how it has led us to create a new way of looking at personal development and leadership, not just in the corporate world, but in life as a whole; not just for businessmen and businesswomen, but for anyone who is interested in learning, growing and developing to produce peak performance, in whatever field they so choose.

This book is also about a passion, one that Marcus and I share. While we agree to disagree on many things, we do have a common passion for fitness, growth and personal development. I remember that someone asked me a question one day: "How would you know that you have made an impact on the people around you?" That question stopped me in my tracks and made me think. I have always wanted to make an impact, but how would I know that I actually have?

For me, the answer is now clear: I have made an impact when I see a person grow, develop and create results that they never thought they could achieve. If they achieve that as the result of my partnership with them, then I can say that I have made an impact of which I can be proud. In contrast to what I see in most of the fitness industry today, I see health and fitness as an outwardly-focussed enterprise, one that allows you to take care of the critical relationships and tasks in your world. The desire to have six-pack abs or big biceps for self-absorbed, aesthetic reasons leaves me cold.

My personal conversation is about how I choose to be growing, developing and learning, standing next to Marcus—because I believe our work is important to this world. At a time when so many people are fighting to be *right*, we aim to support people to be *excellent* and in particular, to support them to become *leaders* and to create leaders around them.

I guess it is not a coincidence that my name is Sari, which means "essence" in Indonesian. I want to honour my name by supporting other people to manifest their essence in the world, because ultimately, that is what I have discovered to be at the heart of *my* essence.

I dedicate this book to that purpose.

THE STRUCTURE OF THIS BOOK

Part I of this book is written by Marcus and contains some key elements of the personal development work that TWP and Newfield Asia (NFA) have used all over the world to support and challenge people to produce peak performance in whatever field they choose. The principles discussed in Part I form the foundation of the drive to produce excellence in your own life and in the lives of other people. It does not matter whether your goal is to be the best parent, athlete or manager you can be, these principles will support you in reaching your goal.

Part II, which is written by Sari, deals with the body, movement, exercise and nutrition, and provides a look at how these elements can all contribute to your personal and leadership development goals. This is where the rubber really begins to hit the road. This part aims to get you challenging yourself physically and starting to think about how movement, nutrition and exercise can help you develop not only your physical state but your emotional and mental states as well.

Part III is where it all comes together. Written by both Marcus and Sari, this part of the book offers a transformed view of leadership by combining all the elements of personal development, body, movement and nutrition discussed in Parts I and II. Historically, these have been very separate areas: movement and exercise work to make you fitter while personal development works to make you smarter. The whole premise of this book is that this separation is a fallacy and that in fact, paying attention to your physical state, your movement and your nutrition can make a huge difference in producing peak performance in *all* areas of your life, not just when it comes to your physical fitness. For too long the world of leadership development was purely focussed on the mental aspect. More recently, the world of emotions has grudgingly been admitted to the party. It is high time that we invite the worlds of the body and movement into the game as well, because as we shall see, they have a huge amount to offer.

LOOKING AHEAD

BY MARCUS & SARI

01

CONNECTING LEADERSHIP AND THE BODY

Leadership. Your body. On first glance, they seem to be two entirely separate things. Leadership is intangible, and involves having a vision and engaging with other people so that they follow you, whilst your body is a physical, tangible and personal thing. The main purpose of this book is to offer a different point of view, namely that your body, how you hold it and move it, is a fundamental part of your leadership. The world of leadership and the world of the physical body are not as separate as they may initially appear.

In fact, the athletic and sporting world has known and embraced these links for some time: athletes and sportspeople have taken on the principles of personal development and leadership much more enthusiastically than business executives and budding leaders have taken on the principles of health and fitness. It is now commonplace for athletes to talk of SMART goals, visualisation techniques and game debriefs, but it is still very rare to hear executives and aspiring leaders talk about the way they move their body, their nutrition plans, their exercise routine or their level of flexibility.

Undoubtedly, there is still some snobbishness at play here: have those sweaty, muscle-bound jocks and quinoa-eating yoga types really got anything to teach a serious MBA graduate or budding business leader? In short, we believe that yes, they have, and in this book we will explore crossovers between these domains that can supercharge your efforts to grow and develop, not just as a leader, but as a human being too.

Because the crossover between these two areas is better received by athletes than business leaders, there are many more books out there that deal with applying personal development thinking to the world of sports. This book therefore largely focuses on the converse: the application of physical movement, nutrition and exercise to the worlds of leadership and personal development.

The two of us have watched our worlds coming closer and closer together in recent years. Sari began as a personal trainer dealing largely with physical fitness and working with people who wanted to lose fat, gain muscle, become more flexible, etc. Marcus began as a leadership development trainer and coach dealing largely with belief systems, thinking patterns, moods and emotions and working with people who wanted to become more effective at learning, developing and growing themselves and other people.

Over time, we started to notice this distinction disappearing. Sari began linking people's physical health with their emotional and mental states. Marcus began incorporating physical elements such as movement and nutrition into his coaching and training. As this integration of physical (or "somatic", from *soma*, Greek for "body"), mental and emotional states accelerated, we formed a company that was focussed squarely on developing this concept: Sarius Performance International (SPI). Our initial thinking was crystallised in the Five Pillars of Performance model that we will outline below and which forms the foundation to the whole book.

THE FIVE PILLARS OF PERFORMANCE

When we first formed SPI, we began with these five pillars as our underlying philosophy: the Internal Pillars, comprising the physical state, mental state, and emotional state; and the External Pillars, consisting of practice and support. In the subsequent years, we have greatly expanded our thinking, with the results of that expansion making up the bulk of this book. However, the original Five Pillars of Performance model serves as a useful foundation for the book because it introduces the key pillars and elements that we will return to time and time again.

The one core belief that underpins all the work we do is that in order to truly grow, develop and flourish, human beings cannot rely solely on their thinking and feeling. In addition to their intellect and their emotions, their physical body and range of motion are also of utmost importance. For so long, the physical state and movement have been excluded from these types of discussions and relegated to the gym and the sports field. We believe that for those looking to really maximise their own development and the development of those around them, the body and the practice of conscious movement can offer significant boosts in performance.

In order for human beings to achieve peak performance, all aspects of their "human-being-ness" need to be taken into account. At SPI, we call such an approach Active Synergy Training and Coaching (see Figure 1.1).

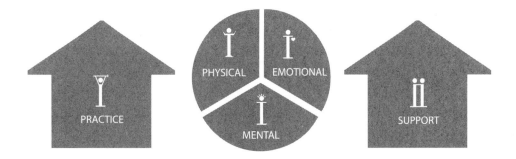

Figure 1.1 SPI's Active Synergy Training and Coaching Model

The Five Pillars of Performance work synergistically to generate sustainable development through a focus on a person's internal system (physical, mental and emotional states) while at the same time working with the external system that surrounds them: their support network and their practice regime. The three Internal Pillars work to *generate* performance, while the two External Pillars work to *sustain* performance. Individually, the Five Pillars of Performance can be summarised as follows:

 ## Physical State Pillar

So many people today see themselves as a brain on a stick and treat other people in a similar manner, especially at work. The body is seen as some kind of necessary evil, an irritating appendage that has to be dragged around in order for the brain to do its work.

However, the body and a person's physical state play a fundamental part in their human growth and development, especially in the domains of learning and knowing, as we shall see later. The body is a key transmitter, receiver and processor of information. Critical elements of the physical state include, but are not limited to: nutrition, energy, breathing, flexibility, strength, power, stability, posture, movement, sleep and restoration. All of these factors are fundamental to peak performance. Rather than seeing the body as an inconvenience, we believe that attending to your body can provide a significant edge not only to your own performance but also to the performance of those whom you seek to lead.

 ## Mental State Pillar

People spend an inordinate amount of time talking to themselves, and most of what is said is unprintable in these pages! The actions that we do or do not take are tightly linked to the beliefs that we have, but we are unaware of the vast majority of these beliefs. This is a recipe for failure and mediocrity. Critical elements of the mental state include, but are not limited to: affirmations, visualisation, beliefs, effective target setting, creating effective self-talk, clarity of purpose and focus.

In Part I of this book we will pay particular attention to how your mental state can either facilitate or impede your performance and the performance of others. A big part of the mental state comes down to language because we communicate with others and with ourselves through the medium of language. In our lives we are always communicating and, as with everything that we repeatedly do, habits begin to form and the resulting patterns become transparent to us. Once our patterns of speech become transparent, we lose sight of them and they come to be seen as "situation normal" or simply "the way things are". It is very difficult to change a habit you do not know you have. This is especially critical with our patterns in language, because, as we shall see, language has the power to shape our reality.

 ## Emotional State Pillar

The English word "emotion" comes from the French word *émouvoir*, which means to stir up. This word in turn comes from the Latin word *emovere*, which means to move out of; *e-* "out" + *movere* "to move". Peak performance, growth and development are not created by intellect alone. Human beings are "moved" to perform (or not) through their emotions. Critical elements of the emotional state include but are not limited to naming, identifying and shifting moods, creating effective emotional states and stress mitigation.

For many people, especially in the corporate world, moods and emotions, like the body, are simply dismissed as irrelevant and inconvenient. They cannot be commanded and controlled and, as such, they are often seen as "dangerous" or "messy". But moods and emotions are critical because they set the frame for what we see as possible in a situation. If you are full of resignation or resentment, then you will see far fewer possibilities than if you are feeling peaceful or enthusiastic.

Support Pillar

Human beings are not islands floating around in some kind of glorious isolation. Rather, we operate in a series of interconnected networks and relationships, and these connections are fundamental enablers or barriers to us achieving what we say we want to achieve. Critical elements regarding support include creating and maintaining networks as well as working with beliefs that can undermine these networks. This is one of the biggest barriers to success that we encounter in our clients. The desire to be Superman or Superwoman is very strong—"I have to prove that I can do everything on my own". Equally strong is the desire to be a nice guy or nice gal—"I don't want to disturb you or be a burden to you".

The top athletes and sportspeople in the world all have coaches, despite the likelihood that they are better players than their coaches. They hire coaches because they are passionate about improving and winning and because they know that however good they are, they cannot "see" themselves in action. Another pair of trusted eyes makes all the difference. Videoing yourself and watching the playback is not the same thing—you are still watching the tape with the same eyes.

Increasingly, the corporate world is waking up to the importance of coaching at senior levels, but it is a slow awakening from what appears to have been a very deep sleep. There are support opportunities all around you, but if you want support, you need to invite it in.

 Practice Pillar

A key element in any drive towards growth, development and learning is the nature of the practice in which people immerse themselves. A key distinction between those who create peak performance and those who produce average results is their practice regime. It is not enough just to practise, rather it is important to pay attention to what it is that you are practising and how you are doing it. Elements of focus include developing and maintaining effective practices.

One of the most common flaws in people's routines is that they end up practising what they enjoy doing. If you just keep focussing on the area that you enjoy, then other areas are going to be neglected; these are often the areas that are holding you back. For a classic example, go to a golf driving range, and look at the number of people pulling off the head cover of an enormous driver and practising their drives over and over again, because they enjoy it more than practising the little chips and pitching shots that everyone knows are the secret to improving your golf score. Moreover, this practice very often goes unsupervised, making it highly likely that these people are simply reinforcing ineffective habits while practising!

Here is a good example of how the External Pillars often interact with each other. If you are willing to engage the *support* of a coach as you *practise* then it can pay huge dividends. In the next chapter, we will go into greater detail on how the individual pillars influence one another, and how you can make them work together to create peak performance.

BUILDING PEAK PERFORMANCE

The Five Pillars of Performance operate as the underlying philosophy throughout our coaching, which will become evident as you read this book. At many points in the book we will return to these pillars and examine more closely the key roles that they all play in personal development and leadership.

To reiterate, your physical, mental and emotional states are all important, and these three Internal Pillars function together to generate performance. Although they are made separate and distinct in our model, in reality they are all closely integrated; if you remove a pillar from a building, do you trust that the building will stay standing for long? In order to develop as a leader, you need to not only be aware of this, but also be able to work with all three of these pillars. However, as we mentioned in Chapter 1, the Internal Pillars on their own can only *generate* peak performance; they cannot *sustain* it. It is only when you are willing to practise effectively and connect to an effective support network that you will be able to sustain the performance generated by the Internal Pillars.

As we shall see, this is true not only for your own performance and development but also when you want to lead or develop other people.

THE INTERNAL PILLARS—GENERATORS OF PERFORMANCE

The Internal Pillars of the physical, mental and emotional states are intimately interrelated. It is very difficult to produce your best performance and to lead others if you only have one or two of these states functioning optimally or if they are pulling in different directions. If one pillar shows any weakness at all, you can be sure that the whole structure will soon collapse on itself. For example:

- You are physically strong enough to accomplish your goal. Mentally, you think your goal is a good idea, but you just do not feel emotionally connected to it;
- You are very passionate about your goal. You think it is achievable, but you just do not have the physical energy to complete the task; or
- You have the physical energy to achieve your goal. You feel passionate about it, but inside, that little voice is telling you, "You cannot do this!"

So many times, it is the one negative element that overcomes the two positive elements! We are programmed to give more attention and credence to the negative element as a way to protect ourselves, as a kind of inbuilt self-defence mechanism.

Often, what then happens is that you get yourself into a negative whirlpool, where these three elements reinforce one another and drag you down in a spiral of non-performance (see Figure 2.1):

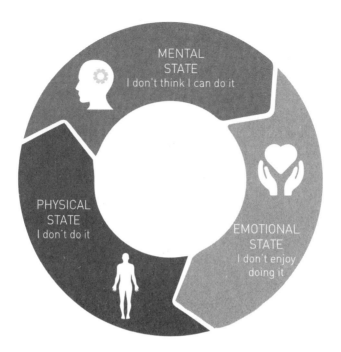

Figure 2.1 The Sarius Spiral of Non-Performance

You don't think you can do it (M).

And because you don't think you can do it,

You don't enjoy doing it (E).

And because you don't enjoy doing it,

You don't do it (P).

And because you don't do it, you tell yourself:

"I can't do it" (M).

And so the spiral repeats.

On the other hand, if you have ever experienced being "in the zone"—this is when you have all three of these states in alignment: you believe you can do the job, you feel passionate about the job, and you have the energy to get the job done. Now, you create a cycle of peak performance (see Figure 2.2):

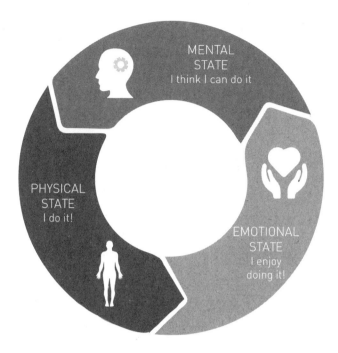

Figure 2.2 The Sarius Spiral of Peak Performance

You think you can do it (M).
And because you think you can do it,
You begin to do it (P).
And because you can do it,
You begin to enjoy doing it (E).
And because you enjoy doing it, you keep doing it and then you tell yourself:
"*I can do it*" (M).

THE EXTERNAL PILLARS—SUSTAINERS OF PERFORMANCE

Support

In our coaching experience, one of the biggest distinguishing factors that we observe between those who succeed and those who do not is the willingness to ask for and accept support.

There is an old proverb that says:

"If you want to go fast, then go alone,
but if you want to go far, then go together."

In the world we live in today, the unwillingness to ask for and accept support is one of the things that never fails to amaze us when we are coaching people. People are surrounded by other people, or even whole departments who would be willing to support them, and yet they insist on doing it all themselves.

The cult of the superhero has much to answer for this—people want to be Superman or Superwoman, and then they wonder why their relationships are all messed up. It is very difficult to be in a relationship with a superhero, and when we come to discuss leadership later in this book, we will see that fundamentally, leadership is a *relationship*: it happens in relationship with other people. It is not a solo endeavour.

Barriers to Receiving Support

In general, we have observed two main reasons why people are reluctant to ask for and accept support. Some people do not want to be a burden; they worry that people are already busy enough and don't have the time or the energy to support them. Other people see asking for and accepting support as a sign of weakness. They have their whole identity wrapped up in their ability to be able to do everything required on their own, and see the need for support as a fundamental flaw in their own character.

A key question to ask yourself at this point is this: What does how you are living your life right now tell you about your attitude towards support? Notice that we did not say "Look at your beliefs about support..." People find it notoriously difficult to truly identify their own beliefs, but if you are willing to look clearly at the results you have in your life right now, then they will give you an indication as to your real attitude and beliefs. This will be a recurring theme in the book.

It is very easy to kid yourself that you have a wonderful and open attitude towards accepting support from others, but if you look at your life and you do not actually have anyone supporting you in a meaningful way, then the chances are that you have some hidden beliefs or attitudes towards support that are holding you back from allowing others to support you.

Practice

Nowadays, almost everyone knows that practice is critical to producing peak performance. Malcolm Gladwell's famous "10,000-Hour Rule" to attain mastery is now well known.[2] However, it is not enough just to keep mindlessly repeating the same tired old practice routines over and over again. *How* you practise is just as critical as the willingness to practise itself.

You probably know the first half of the famous saying: "Practice makes perfect…", but do you know the second half: "…so be careful what you practise"? For a perfect example, visit a gym anywhere in the world, and you will see people enthusiastically practising bad habits over and over again and then wondering why they are developing injuries and postural imbalances!

Practice does not just refer to something that you do in order to develop a skill. Rather, instead, consider that you are *practising* whenever you do something, anything, repeatedly. So, if you drink six cups of coffee every day, that is what you are practising and, hey presto, you get very good at drinking six cups of coffee a day. Practice does indeed make perfect!

Creating Practices

Closely linked to the willingness to practise is the willingness to create practices. Practices are a key part of any coaching program. Our good friend and Director of Training at NFA, Terrie Lupberger, puts it very well in her upcoming book *You Are What You Practice*:

> Helping people generate new results, futures and outcomes is at the core of our work as coaches, leaders and change agents. We encourage new thinking, perspectives, and paradigms. Our questions and observations can generate new awareness in others

---

2   Gladwell first developed the "10,000-Hour Rule" in his book *Outliers* in 2008.

that a particular habit—either in their way of thinking or in their way of behaving—isn't working any longer.

Unfortunately, we human beings have become short-sighted and demanding of quick-fixes. We have immediate, 24/7 access to information. We are inundated with data and overwhelmed with complexity. We want sound bites. We privilege formulaic approaches. We want answers and solutions—fast.

And that's the problem. As much as we would like the quick fix, there just isn't an instant "how-to" for changing thinking and behaviors, so we can get new results. That's where practices and practising comes in. They are the key to change.

A practice is defined as something that you do with the aim of building *capacity*. It is not linked to a specific goal or target. So, for example, in order to develop a capacity for assertiveness, you might adopt the practice of attending boxing classes twice a week. You are not aiming to become the heavyweight champion of the world, but you are looking to develop and embody a capacity for assertiveness.

Marcus goes to the gym on average five times a week, but he is not looking to be Mr Olympia or win any competitions. He goes five times a week because, amongst other things, he is looking to build a capacity of discipline and commitment. There are other capacities that he is also seeking to build; these capacities will become evident later in Part III of the book when we discuss movement and its links to leadership.

There are classic practices, such as yoga or meditation that aim at building basic capacities such as flexibility and peace. However, it is important to be aware that there is no *inherent* link between a practice and a capacity. So, for example, a yoga practice may be aimed at developing flexibility and relaxation, but not necessarily; a yoga practice can easily be adopted to develop a capacity of resilience or stability instead. Moreover, it is also perfectly possible, based on Marcus's personal experience, to practise experiencing tension and frustration by attending yoga classes! As we shall see, the critical element is to be aware and conscious of the specific quality you are intending to build as you practise, and then to focus on that quality while you practise.

CLIENT CASE STUDY

Amit Sevak, former CEO of Laureate Education, South Asia, working with Marcus

After attending one of the programmes at NFA, Amit realised that he had gotten stuck on a plateau and was feeling rather uninspired. He had created a successful career for himself but found that he had lost the original energy that led to his initial success. Upon making this discovery, Amit decided to take up boxing as an attempt to kickstart his system.

It only took a few sessions before Amit found himself rediscovering that old drive he thought he had lost. When we caught up some months later, Amit told me that he had since signed up for another 20 sessions with his boxing coach. He now recognises the interconnectedness between his physical, mental and emotional states, and how they influence his overall productivity at work. The physical practice of boxing helps him develop the capacity for mental focus, which inspires him and provides him the drive to achieve his future goals and bring his career to the next level.

Very often, in order to maximise effectiveness, the pillars of support and practice go hand-in-hand. If you are willing to practise while allowing yourself to also be supported by an expert or a "master" in the appropriate discipline, then you stand a real chance of attaining peak performance.

PERSONAL REFLECTION

Sari: Practice and Support

As we mention, the pillars of practice and support often go hand-in-hand, but like a lot of people, I prefer one to the other! I have never had a problem with practising. All through my life, people have told me that I am very determined. Although I cannot really see that for myself, I can recognise that I am very single-minded whenever I have a goal in mind.

I started working out and became a personal trainer when Marcus and I moved to Hong Kong in 2008. When we moved to Singapore in 2010, I started working out a lot more regularly. As usual, I wanted to push myself as hard as possible, and so I started looking into competing in fitness physique competitions. I was already practising hard, but when I saw the athletes against whom I would be competing, I knew I had to step up my game. So, I did what I always do: I simply practised harder. I read the best books and went to the gym six days a week to put into practice what I was reading.

However, it did not take me long to realise that what I was doing was not going to be enough. Although I was practising hard, what I was practising was not going to get me where I wanted to go. I hated to admit it, but I had to face the truth: if I was going to do well or even stand a chance of winning in these competitions, I was going to need to enlist some support, and not just any support. I needed to find an expert, or as it turned out, in this case, two experts. I found Singapore's foremost bodybuilders, Augustine Lee and Joan Liew of The Fitness Factory. While I did not want to be a bodybuilder, I did need to work with people who had experience in working with the body competitively. These would be people who knew just what to focus on in order to win physique competitions.

At first, I resisted the whole process; I had always trained by myself, and having someone tell me how to do it felt strange and uncomfortable. But it didn't take me long to realise something important: I was more interested in winning than in being right about my own knowledge and ability to coach myself through the whole process. When I surrendered to being supported by these experts, not only did my enjoyment of the process increase by leaps and bounds, but I also noticed my learning was massively accelerated and I became even more emotionally attached to my goal.

Although I had been determined before I met Augustine and Joan, I found the whole experience of accepting support from a "master trainer" very liberating. Suddenly, I had somebody to hold me accountable in a way that I had not been able to do for myself. In addition, I fed off their certainty; they believed in me, and because of their experience, I felt my confidence levels rise immeasurably.

Even though I often present a confident front to the world, like anybody else I do have my fears and doubts. It worked for me in a counter-intuitive way: Initially, I was reluctant to accept support because I thought I needed to prove I could do it all myself to keep my confidence high. However, my confidence started waning when I realised that my own practice regime was not going to be enough. It was actually when I opened up and accepted support that my confidence started to grow.

However, it was not simply Augustine and Joan's support that helped me, it was also how they changed the way I practised. Although they acknowledged that I was practising very hard, they made it clear to me that my exercise and nutritional practices were simply not going to help me reach the required standards for the new game that I had chosen to play. They came at the problem from a totally different perspective.

I learned a lot from this whole experience. In particular, I realised the massive impact that accepting support and being willing to switch up your practice can make. However, it also became clear that it was the choice of purpose and my emotional connection to it that was the key. If I had simply wanted to become a little fitter, then I did not really need to make these changes. It was only once I decided to compete in fitness physique competitions that everything changed. I'm happy to say it had the desired effect.

03

MOVE YOUR BODY, MOVE YOUR LIFE

The Five Pillars of Performance outlined in the previous chapters are the fundamental elements that underpin the drive to develop yourself and your leadership and ultimately, produce peak performance. We will be expanding further on these themes as the book progresses. However, even at this stage, you can see that the *body* is a fundamental enabler to creating peak performance, not just in the domains of sporting endeavour and physical activity, but rather in *any* domain. Strength, energy and the willingness to physically practise are all critically important. However, this is only part of the story, as will become evident later in the book.

While this is a book about leadership, it is not leadership in the traditional hierarchical understanding of the word. The hierarchical model is very simple and sounds like this: "I have one more stripe on my arm than you do, therefore you must do what I say, or else there will be consequences." While this is rarely explicitly stated, it is the implicit driver behind a vast amount of human interaction, in and out of the office: the idea of "Do it or else". This is called being "the boss" and while it might seem very quick and easy, it is very limited in its ability to produce long-term, sustainable excellence for you or the people around you.

In contrast, the kind of leadership we will be discussing in this book involves the distinction of someone *choosing* to follow someone else (without the fear of reprisal if they choose not to). Also notice that this distinction is by no means confined to the corporate world. For example, do your children (or your spouse) follow you because you have the title of "parent" (or "spouse"), or do they follow you because they choose to do so, based on how you show up in the world? It is a challenging question for you to ask yourself.

As already stated, one of the big drivers for both of us to write this book was the observation that for most people, these two domains are entirely separate. If they want to move better, then they hire a personal trainer (like Sari), go to yoga classes or read fitness books; if they want to develop personally or as a leader, then they hire a coach/trainer (like Marcus) or they buy self-development books. The essence of this book is to show that in fact, these two domains are not only linked, they can actually powerfully inform each other. There are practices in the domain of the physical body, movement and exercise that will have a huge impact in your capacity to achieve great results in all areas of your life and leadership in particular. This realisation has become ever clearer since we founded SPI in 2011. It was here that we began to see an increasing number of connections between the worlds of personal development and movement. Instead of simply offering physical training in a PT session, Sari started adding key fundamentals of personal development into the mix, and clients immediately began to experience something different.

CLIENT CASE STUDY

Victoria Mander, Head of Content & Proposal Management, TB Global Sales at Standard Chartered Bank, working with Sari

Victoria came to me as most people do: with the main goal of improving their physical state. Like many of the corporate executives I meet, Victoria had noticed that she was gradually doing less and less exercise and movement, and her initial goal was to lose some weight and improve her flexibility. However, as we worked on her goal with some classic physical exercises, Victoria started to notice that their impact was not confined to her physical state. She began to feel different and think different, especially with regard to herself and her leadership.

I came to learn that Victoria was determined and motivated towards exercise, but only when she was going through an exercise phase. However, these phases came and went, never quite seeming to stick. Through our sessions, I also found out that Victoria felt frustrated with her work; she hadn't attained the seniority she wanted, and she could never quite put her finger on what was holding her back.

Over the years, we realised that Victoria's approaches to work and exercise were very similar. She was inconsistently determined when it came to exercising, and it was the same when it came to her work. Victoria has since come to understand that her main issue is about feeling in control of herself. Our physical training sessions, which were initially focussed on developing stability (more on that in Part III), have since helped her improve her posture, her energy levels, as well as her physical appearance, which has resulted in better self-esteem and emotional stability. Most importantly, Victoria has learnt that consistent determination is what gives her that feeling of control in her life, whether it comes to work or exercise. She has begun to regain and retain the awareness of how it feels to be in control of her physical body. This embodiment of control is something that has carried over into her work as well: she finally got that promotion she was going for.

After rediscovering that sense of control over both her physical fitness and her work, Victoria has come to realise that as long as she is in control of her physical, mental and emotional states, she can deliver her best and become the best leader she can be.

The difference that Victoria has experienced in working with Sari has been mirrored in many of her other clients. Something special and synergistic starts to happen when you begin to interact with the complete human being in front of you, rather than simply focussing on one piece of them, such as their physical condition. Improvements in one area, such as posture, can have a huge impact on another area, such as determination. It is the feedback from many clients like Victoria that has been one of the drivers for us to write this book.

**OVERVIEW:
SELF-REFLECTION**

As you read this book, it will be useful to keep a pen nearby. At the end of each part, we will ask you to reflect on how the part relates to your own experience. If you are committed to getting the most you can out of this book, then we strongly urge you to make it an interactive reading experience. This will only be effective, however, if you are willing to be honest with yourself and base your answers on the results that you see in your life, rather than the justifications and explanations that you see in your head.

Support

Take a moment to reflect on and note down what you see in your life with regards to support.

1. The people I allow to support me in my life:

2. I allow these people to support me because:

3. The people I do not allow to support me in my life:

4. I do not allow these people to support me because:

5. The areas of my life in which I allow myself to be supported:

6. I allow myself to be supported in these areas because:

7. The areas of my life in which I do not allow myself to be supported:

8. I do not allow myself to be supported in these areas because:

Practice

Now turn your attention to what you practise (or do repeatedly) in your everyday life. Remember to note down what you are *really* practising, not what you imagine practising in your mind.

1. What I am practising in my life:

2. What I am unwilling to practise in my life:

3. The areas where I am currently on track to achieve my purpose:

4. The areas where I am currently not on track to achieve my purpose:

5. What my *results* are telling me about where my practice is effective and where it is ineffective:

Now think about your practices. A practice is something that you do in order to develop a certain capacity. It is not an action step towards a specific goal.

6. The practices that I have developed in my life and the capacities I am seeking to develop as a result are:

7. The capacities that it would benefit me to develop in my life are:

8. The potential practices that I could adopt as a way to develop these capacities are:

PART I

PERSONAL DEVELOPMENT

BY MARCUS

04

THE CHALLENGE OF DEVELOPMENT

If you are reading this book, then it is highly likely that this is not the first personal development, leadership development or self-help book that you have picked up... and yet, here you are again! If all these self-help books actually worked, then why do people keep writing and buying them? They do so because these books don't work! Wouldn't life be great if all you needed to do was to read a book or Google the necessary information? Actually, it probably would not be so great after all, because life happens most powerfully in the *process* of attaining goals, rather than at the moment that you actually attain them, but that is another story for another time in another self-help book.

Self-help books give you the knowledge to "help yourself", and we are all brought up to believe that when we have the knowledge or the know-how, we will be able to produce the desired result. However, there is evidence all around us that this is not the case. America (and increasingly, the Western world in general) has a huge amount of knowledge about diet and nutrition, but at the same time it also has a huge proportion of people who are overweight and want to weigh less. Why? Because other things are more important: guy gets home from work, he wants to lose weight, he *knows* that a chicken salad would be the best choice for that goal, but he has had a bad day at work and so he chooses a burger and fries, because in that moment, feeling comfortable (a theme we shall return to at length!) is more important than losing weight.

However, this is only half the story.

LISTENING

The other reason this book will not work is that human beings are horrible listeners.

Now, look at what you just did with that last statement: "human beings are horrible listeners". Chances are that you did what 95% of the world's population will do when given such a statement: you either agreed with it, or you disagreed with it. That is how human beings have evolved to listen: agree or disagree and then move on. However, neither of these options are very effective if you are looking to develop and grow.

Imagine yourself as a box of "X's"—where the "X's" represent all your beliefs, attitudes, points of view, experiences, etc.

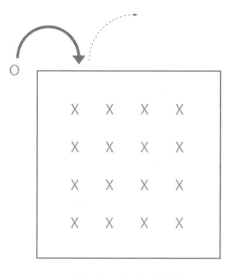

AGREE / DISAGREE

Figure 4.1 The Agree/Disagree Model

Now imagine someone giving you a different point of view, an "O", if you like. What choices do you have?

1. Agree with it: this statement is "right", ie. it is consistent with one of your existing "X's".

2. Disagree with it: the statement is "wrong", ie. it is inconsistent with your current "X's". When you do this, you are basically erecting a force field around your box of "X's" to keep the "O" out. You may do it forcefully through argument and pushing back or you may do it subtly by changing the subject or ignoring it, but the result is the same: the "O" never gets close to entering your box of "X's" (see Figure 4.1).

3. Analyse or assess it: this seems sensible, right? You are a sensible, rational 21st-century human being, so you think about it, you assess it. However, when you do this, what are you assessing the "O" against? What criteria are you using, to see if it is a "good" point of view or not? Your "X's"! And guess what? The "O" does not look like your "X", so it ends up in the trash can anyway.

4. Sophisticated analysis: this is the subtle version of option number 3. After an initial analysis, once you see that the "O" does not fit, you deconstruct it, manipulate it, and then rebuild it, so that it looks like, you guessed it, an "X"! Yay! You let it in! But did you really? No, you took a different point of view and twisted it until it mirrored a point of view that you already had, and only then did you let it in.

After all of these options, your box of "X's" looks exactly the same as it did before! For most people, as they get older, the walls of their box become higher and thicker and the "X's" become "<u>X</u>'s". This is why children learn and develop so much quicker than adults: the walls of their box are very low and thin, they don't have many "X's" and the ones that they do have are "ₓ's". Unlike adults, children are more interested in developing and growing than they are in defending what they already know.

Being Open

There is a fifth option: just to let the "O" in, and to let it sit there in the box as an "O", a different point of view sitting in your box of "X's". This requires you to give up your snap judgements of "agree/disagree" and to be *open*. This is very counter-cultural in the 21ˢᵗ century—where everything has become about speed and fast decision making. Instead of rushing to a decision and then tweeting about it, you actually just allow a different point of view in, and let it sit there, even if it is in contradiction to your original point of view.

If you do *that*, then look what happens to your box (see Figure 4.2):

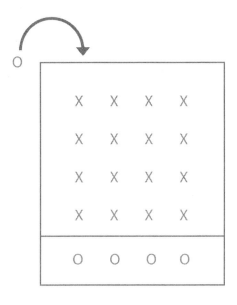

ALLOW / ACCEPT

Figure 4.2 The Allow/Accept Model, Step 1

Being open gives you a space in which you can choose how to respond, rather than just making snap judgements based on your history, habits and what makes you comfortable. If you then use this space to assess the "O" based on the question, "Would keeping this 'O' help me get closer to my goal?", then you are on your way to producing the results you say you want to produce. If you choose to keep the "O" then it eventually becomes… an "X", and look what then happens to your box (see Figure 4.3):

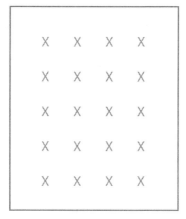

ALLOW / ACCEPT

Figure 4.3 The Allow/Accept Model, Step 2

Now, your box is bigger! That is real growth. In comparison, merely continuing to add more and more "X's" to your box will not make it grow. This is because adding more "X's" cannot be considered real development; you are simply reinforcing your existing points of view.

So, look back at two of the statements already contained in this book:

- Fitness and nutrition are integral to personal development and leadership.
- Human beings are horrible listeners.

Notice how you responded to these statements. Were you open to them or did you instantly agree/disagree and move on?

Agree/Disagree

If you agree with 100% of the things written in this book and yet are still not leading effectively, then something else is going on. Just like our tired burger-eating fellow, you have the knowledge but are not using it because something else is more important to you, such as being comfortable. If you disagree with 100% of the things written in this book, then congratulations! I am not invested in my "O's" being *right*. You are welcome to be right about your "X's", but then you need to ask yourself: are they really working for you? If you keep them, will they maximise your physical, mental and emotional states and support you in becoming the most effective leader you could possibly be? Ultimately, you need to ask yourself this question: why did you even pick up this book in the first place? Do you just want to be right? After all, being right is one of the most addictive drugs in human history!

If you really do want to use this book effectively, then my suggestion is to pay attention to how you read it, and whether you are willing to be *open* as you do so. In particular, pay attention to any "O's" that you want to violently prevent from breaching your wall of "X's". In my experience, it is the "O's" that you resist the most that contain the most value. As a way to start, consider how open you were to the whole idea of "X's" and "O's" in this chapter.

The importance of being open in order to learn, develop and grow is a fundamental part of much of my coaching. Of course, people do not go around consciously saying to themselves, "I want to be closed today", it often just becomes a habit fuelled by position and experience: "I don't need to be open to input because I am the boss (or the parent) and I have more experience." This kind of attitude becomes transparent after a time, and you carry around a fixed box of "X's" that you unconsciously hold as "right". But very often, people who have become close-minded in this way are also completely unaware of that fact. How, then, do you become aware of your own blind spots?

CLIENT CASE STUDY

Vinod Tiwari, COO of the Pulp Business with Aditya Birla Group, working with Marcus

Vinod sought my help to improve his working relationship with his team. He could see that his relationships with his team members were not deep enough to hit his stretching targets. After observing him at work, I realised that Vinod was practising a very prevalent attitude, one we term "blindness": he felt that he was generally right, while some of his team members would often express opposing opinions. He would ask his team to achieve lofty goals, but their differences in opinion often left them unable to reach these goals.

The impact of an attitude of blindness rarely remains confined to the Mental State Pillar. Once it becomes second nature to defend your "X's" in the domain of the Mental State Pillar, you begin to manifest transparent habits in the domains of the Emotional and Physical State Pillars as well. In the Emotional State Pillar, certain moods and emotions (notably anger) become more prevalent than others, while some others (notably gratitude) completely disappear. Similarly, in the Physical State Pillar, certain physical habits and postures (notably tightness) become habitual, while others (notably looseness) disappear. Once I noticed that Vinod was consistently displaying these emotional and physical habits, I was able to diagnose the main reason for his stagnation: he had become close-minded and blind to the opinions of others.

Naturally, it took a while for Vinod to acknowledge his attitude of blindness, but eventually he had the courage to tell the truth about his situation even though it was not very flattering. Once he came to terms with this, Vinod decided to change his attitude by eliciting feedback from others and looking at situations from perspectives other than his own. He soon found himself seeing new and different options and building deeper relationships with his team members in the process. Vinod's newfound rapport with his team has allowed him to make bigger requests of them at work, requests that they are now willing to grant. Moving forward together with his team in this way has led to greater success not only for Vinod, but also his team and his business unit as a whole.

Vinod was able to discover his blind spot because he was open and trusting enough to listen to feedback from an outside party. As a senior manager it can take a lot of courage to listen to honest feedback and act on it. In Part III, we will look more closely at the importance of feedback.

FOUR KEY QUESTIONS OF PERSONAL DEVELOPMENT

If you came to this book looking for answers, then you might be disappointed. One thing that characterises our approach to personal development is a belief in powerful questions that are asked by the trainer/coach. The role of the "player" (in this case, you!) is to honestly answer the questions posed.

We will start off with the four key questions of personal development: "Who am I?", "Where am I?", "Where do I want to go?" and finally, "What stops me getting there?" Exploring these four questions will provide insight into how the three Internal Pillars of Performance are inextricably integrated. The questions show up in the domain of the Mental State Pillar and yet you will see how your mental state influences and is influenced by your Emotional and Physical State Pillars. Your answers to these questions have a profound impact on how you feel and how you hold your body. Similarly, how you feel and how you move your body will have a big impact on how you answer these questions.

05

WHO AM I?

In a book on leadership and movement, you might be surprised to see this as the first question to consider. A more traditional approach would be to start off by giving you advice on what you need to do in order to become a better leader or to improve your movement. But this is not a traditional book! Rather than wade in with some advice (that you most likely already know but are not applying), let's instead start by taking a look at what you have already decided about yourself. The question "Who am I?" is one of the most fundamental and powerful questions of all, and answering it is a critical first step because it is the foundation of everything that comes next. It is the starting point of your journey.

The statement "I am…" is a big one, because it is a declaration concerning your identity. Once you have decided that you *are/are not* something, it becomes much harder to change it. For example, once you have labelled yourself as a "shy" person, it becomes much harder to go out and meet people. Why? Because you have created a public identity that involves being shy. This is now what other people *expect* of you, and it is also what *you* expect of yourself. This also gives you a great justification for not going out to meet people: "It's just not me".

Once you have decided that you are good or bad at something, the tendency is to go through life finding more evidence to support what you have decided about yourself. Much of what happens in your life is created by you wanting to act in accordance with what you have already decided about who you are. If, however, you see speaking up and meeting people as something you simply find comfortable or uncomfortable to do, then it becomes a lot easier to change this behaviour if you so choose.

ASSERTIONS AND ASSESSMENTS

Notice there are two fundamentally different types of "I am" statements that look deceptively similar:

- I am a man.
- I am tall.

The former is what Fernando Flores identified as an assertion: it is verifiable; it is either true or false; it tells you about the object being described (in this case, me); it is historical in nature (I was a man before I said it); and, on its own, it does not generate much in the future.[3] The latter is what Flores identified as an assessment: it is neither true *nor* false; it is not verifiable (although it may be grounded or ungrounded); it tells you everything about my standards regarding

---

3   I first became aware of the distinction between assessments and assertions in Fernando Flores' work *Conversations for Action and Collected Essays* through the NFA Ontological Learning Program. However, the initial concept of the speech acts and the generative nature of language dates back to the philosophers J.L. Austin and J.R. Searle.

height but it tells you nothing about me physically. You still have no idea if I am 5 feet and 5 inches tall or 6 feet and 5 inches tall!

Assessments are very "sticky" and, unlike assertions, tend to be predictive of the future, because as human beings, we love to be *right*, and once we have decided that we *are* or *are not* a certain way, then we like to prove ourselves right over and over again.

The final thing that is interesting to notice about assessments is that they exist independent of facts! I can say "I am tall" whatever my height, and never be wrong (or right). In reality, I am 6 feet and 2 inches tall. Would you consider that "tall"? That would depend on your standards regarding height. For example, a Dutch person's standards regarding height are rather different to a Singaporean's standards. Neither is right nor wrong. "Tall" is an assessment. It depends on the standards of the person doing the assessing. In contrast, height is an assertion. "I am 6 feet and 2 inches tall" is verifiable. It is true or false. It is not dependent on my (or anyone else's) standards.

It can be very rewarding to pay close attention to how you link your assessments to your assertions. For example, "I am a man" is an assertion, and on its own is not very generative of the future. However, the assessments that I tack on to my assertion become extremely predictive of the future! You can see how it all comes together:

Assertion: I am a man.

Because I am a man,

I can be angry.
I cannot cry.

I must be strong.
I must not be vulnerable.

I need to be in charge.
I don't need to listen to others.

Men are breadwinners.
Men are not financially dependent on women.

Even though I start out with a single verifiable assertion, I can quickly generate a whole slew of assessments that follow on from that one assertion. In this example, the assertion "I am a man" quickly leads to many assessments which are extremely restrictive and predictive of my future and the future of the people around me. This is why it helps to become aware of the assessments that you are linking to your assertions.

Assertions are not better than assessments. There is nothing wrong or bad about assessments. The problem arises when you confuse the two. Once you begin to hold an assessment as though it is an assertion, not only do you become stuck in a prison of your own making, you put other people in prisons too. For example, if someone you have decided is "unreliable" arrives on time, then you either ignore this example of punctuality or explain it away ("Ah, that is just because...") and carry on holding your assessment of unreliability regardless.

Once again, as was the case when we examined "X's" and "O's" in Chapter 4, human beings love to be right even when the evidence right before our eyes contradicts our assessment.

06

WHERE AM I?

This is the heart of the work that we do in our leadership development workshops. We begin by asking one of my favourite personal development questions: what are the key things you need to know if you are going to embark on a successful journey? Most likely, your list would include things such as a destination, a budget, resources (time, money, etc.), a mode of transport, an itinerary, a purpose (why are you going?), a backup plan, a strategy, a view of possible obstacles, etc. These are all important elements, but there is one critical element missing.

Imagine I gave you a map to make the journey. What is the one thing you still need in order to make use of the map?

You need to know your current location. From which point are you starting?

This is so obvious that it usually gets overlooked. Everyone thinks they are clear about their starting point, but in reality, nothing could be further from the truth! Human beings are hopeless at recognising their starting point.

Let's look at an example to see what happens when we fail to accurately identify our starting point (see Figure 6.1):

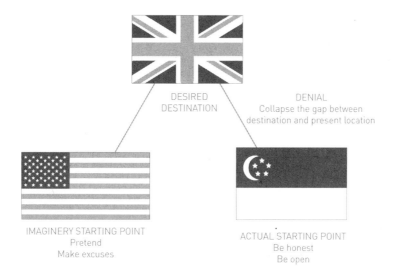

DESIRED
DESTINATION

DENIAL
Collapse the gap between
destination and present location

IMAGINERY STARTING POINT
Pretend
Make excuses

ACTUAL STARTING POINT
Be honest
Be open

Figure 6.1 A Tale of Three Cities: Misidentifying Your Starting Point

In this example, I am in Singapore and my desired destination is London. But I think that Los Angeles is better than Singapore, so I like to tell myself that I am in Los Angeles instead. I deny that I am in Singapore and pretend that I am in Los Angeles. Why? Because it is easier to think that I am in Los Angeles: I look better if I am there, and Los Angeles is closer to London than Singapore is. So I produce stories and justifications that make it look as if I am in Los Angeles even though I am actually in Singapore.

HONESTY

Very often my coaching sessions begin with exactly these kinds of discussions. I ask my client about their health and their first answer is usually "fine" (denial), and then after further discussion, they usually admit that something is up (high blood pressure, bad back, overweight, etc.). But what comes next is the kicker. They say something like this:

"OK, I admit it, I am overweight… but I am only overweight because of these long hours, the travel and the business lunches and dinners!"

So, what they want me to believe is that the only reason they are overweight is their *job* and so if it was not for the *job*, then they would weigh 10 kg less! However, that is a total smokescreen: it is perfectly possible to work in that job *and* weigh 10 kg less!

In other words, they like to live in the illusion that they are in Los Angeles (living a healthy life), when the truth is that they are in Singapore (living unhealthily). By doing this, it allows them to protect their image and keep doing what they are doing. However, all this time they are not getting any closer to London (being healthy)!

The same thing occurs with relationships. In the first conversation, my client says their relationships are "fine" and then as we progress, the story changes and they admit that their relationship with their spouse, children or parents is strained (or worse), and they want to sell me the story that this situation only exists because of their job or some other excuse. This version of the story allows them to protect their image of being a great spouse/parent/child. However, this version also keeps them stuck, because as long as they blame the job for the state of their relationships, they are doomed. Once again, it is perfectly possible to have a job *and* have great relationships, as long as you are willing to be honest about the fact that it is *you* who is creating the current state of your relationships, not your job!

However, this does not mean that you should start blaming *yourself* instead. This strategy leads to the same destination—you get stuck. It is perfectly possible for you to create the relationships and health that you desire. However, as we will explore below, while it is possible for you, it may not be possible for your public identity or image!

Bottom line: if you are not honest about where you start from in life, then you are doomed in any attempt to reach your desired destination.

IMAGE

Telling the truth about your starting point often requires courage. You have to be willing to give up your image as a "good" person (whatever you think that means).

Most people hate to do that, because they think it means they are admitting that how they are currently living their life is bad or wrong in some way. This is not the case. It is perfectly possible to be honest about how you are really living your life without making yourself wrong, or beating yourself up about it.

People often have a lot invested in their image and their pretense that they are in Los Angeles and so do not want to get real about where they are in their life. In Chapter 9, I will go into more detail about common images people take on and how they can hold you back from achieving your goals.

AS IS AND TO BE, INTANGIBLE AND TANGIBLE

Everyone likes to focus on the destination and "the vision thing", and while that certainly is important, trying to get to get that point without stopping to clearly establish your starting point in life is a very common trap. The As Is/To Be & Intangible/Tangible Matrix (Figure 6.2) illustrates the issue clearly:

TO BE	**VISION**	**TARGETS**
AS IS	**CONTEXT / CULTURE**	**RESULTS**
	INTANGIBLE	**TANGIBLE**

- Be clear on "AS IS" before you set visions or goals
- Take ownership of your results (no excuses!) and they will illuminate your context or culture.

Figure 6.2 As Is/To Be & Intangible/Tangible Matrix

In general, people are far more comfortable talking about the "To Be" state (how things will be in the future) than talking about the "As Is" state (how things are right now). On the intangible side, this means talking about the vision, while on the tangible side, this means talking about goals and targets.

It is far easier and more comfortable to discuss the desired future than it is to responsibly examine the truth of the current reality. As we have already seen, human beings are not too keen to tell the truth about where they currently are and how they came to be there; they would rather find stories and excuses to explain away their results. Similarly, it is very difficult to clearly see the current culture (personal or team) while you are in it.

This was something I encountered when I moved to Indonesia after 30 years of living in England. Many things that I had taken for granted over decades were suddenly up for question. I suddenly became aware of many things I did not even know I assumed and believed in. It was initially a rather destabilising period, but one for which I am forever grateful. I became the archetypal fish scooped out of the fish bowl and left on the table for a while; suddenly after all those years I knew what water was, and in a very real way, not just as a concept!

While it is true that all four boxes on this matrix are important, it is critical that you are able to establish a ground zero for the "As Is" state. If you are able to do that, and then set clear and specific goals as well as a motivating vision, then you have a real shot at producing the change that you say you want: the "To Be" state.

ENTITLEMENT

There is a major factor that links the first two questions ("Who am I?" and "Where am I?") with the following one ("Where do I want to go?"). This is a factor that I have seen stand in the way of more people seeking to achieve peak performance than almost any other. This factor is entitlement, which means "that to which I have a right". It is not just who you have decided you are that matters, but also what you have assessed you are therefore entitled to do, or not do as a result.

In recent years, this has become one of the most pervasive limiting assessments that I see when I am coaching. Although it is rarely spoken—people do not often go around saying: "I am entitled to do/not do that"—it is a very common assessment that undercuts their capacity for effective action. Notice that as with every assessment, although it seems to show up in the domain of the Mental State Pillar, it is affected by and has significant effects on the Emotional and Physical State Pillars. A specific belief about entitlement is inevitably linked to certain emotions, postures and body shapes.

There are many reasons why someone might start to assess themselves as entitled to a certain behaviour or status. The most common reasons come from a position held or a length of time served, for example:

"I am a Director now, so…"
"I have worked in this company for 10 years, so…"
"I am the father/mother/eldest child/breadwinner of this family, so…"
"I have been working hard all week, so…"

This sense of entitlement comes from an assessment that you have done something that has earned you the right to do, or not do, something else. The feeling is also comparative: "I have done something and *they have not*". What we tell ourselves is that if/when the other person has done as much as we have, then they too would be entitled to the same benefit. This is often linked to a sense of "earning your stripes" or "paying your dues".

Usually, when you believe yourself to be entitled to something, you have a logical reason to justify that belief. After all, if you are a senior manager and have worked in the business for 10 years, do you not have rights and privileges that a new management trainee does not share?

This is where the breakdown begins: it may well be the case that your past history has earned you certain "rights" in the company or family with regard to what you are expected to do or not do, but when you are faced with a choice between exercising those rights and being effective, which will you choose?

A surprising number of people will choose the former option. They see that if they do something "below their pay grade", there is the possibility of success, maybe even a major one, but what gets in the way is their notion of entitlement and their concept of "fairness". For example, you might hear this:

> *"Sure, I know I could stay back at the office to finish this report, but that is no longer my job. I used to do that when I was a junior manager, and now, I'm a senior manager. It is not fair to expect me to still do that, and I'm entitled not to do it—just look at my title."*

The consequence is that the results suffer, sacrificed on the altar of righteousness. It has become more important to be right than to achieve the best possible result.

The "rights" to which you believe you are entitled may be enshrined in a contract, or they may simply be unspoken expectations that live in your head. Both are barriers to being effective, but the latter is especially difficult for others to work with, as people rarely have any idea as to what your unspoken expectations actually are.

What makes "entitlement" especially combustible is the mood that often accompanies it: "righteous indignation". Such a combination can make a person very difficult to work with, as they are either likely to explode, without warning, from the perceived injustice of it all, or simply clam up and take the attitude of, "Well if you can't figure out the problem here, then I'm not going to tell you". The mood that an assessment of entitlement kills, is that of gratitude.

So, what is the alternative? The first step is to recognise it in yourself when it arises (and it surely will, at some point in your life). Once you become aware of it, then you have the possibility of making a different choice. You cannot change something that you cannot see. This is why our work generally begins by asking you to look at *yourself*: learning to see things in yourself is the critical but often overlooked first step before you can learn to work with others. Coaches and clients both have things to which we are "blind"; it is part of the human condition.

The second step is to ask yourself what you want to achieve in the situation that you are facing: do you want to be right about your assessment of entitlement or do you want to be effective? Are you willing to take a responsible attitude to the results around you, or are you instead going to focus on your "rights" in the situation? If you are currently experiencing any frustration in life with regard to your results or your relationships, check in with yourself and see if there is a notion of entitlement lurking somewhere in there. It is one of the biggest barriers to being effective.

It is also possible that you might develop a pattern of feeling disentitled, which often sounds like this: "I do not deserve happiness, success, love, etc." While it might look like the complete opposite of a sense of entitlement, a belief of disentitlement can be equally disempowering and just as sticky.

As we shall see later in this book, one of the key things that people today like to feel entitled to is comfort. Their conversation sounds like this:

> *"I have progressed to a point in my life where I am now entitled not to experience the 'discomfort' that I used to experience."*

This, as we shall see, has far-reaching consequences if you are genuinely interested in learning, growing and developing and/or leading others.

07

WHERE DO I WANT TO GO?

At first glance, this seems like the easiest question to answer, right? You just need to set down what you want—then you can worry about how to achieve it later. Not so fast!

GOALS

When I am working with people as a coach, I am constantly amazed at how often people are either working on goals that are so vague as to be unworkable or working on goals they are not actually invested in. The whole concept of SMART goals is well established and I will not spend time on it here, except to say that clarity on what you want, by when, is critical. The more clarity you have, the clearer you can see if you are on or off track.

However, every goal has two elements: the tangible (represented by the Mental State Pillar in the Five Pillars of Performance model: "What I think I want") and the intangible (represented by the Emotional State Pillar: "Why I want it"). While the tangible "what", "how many" and "by when" are important and usually prioritised, they are not in fact the secret to producing results. The decisive element lies on the intangible side: namely "Why you want it", and in particular, the experience/feeling you are looking to create.

Consider this: if I was to ask you whether you want the following, then what would you say?

- The latest Mercedes Benz sports car?
- A luxury villa in Bali?
- $10 million in the bank?

Chances are that you would say yes to at least one of the options above. However, here is the shocker: no, you don't. You don't really want any of them!

What you really want is the intangible emotional experience that you say *goes with* those tangible objects. Maybe you associate the sports car with a sense of attractiveness, recognition or sex appeal. Maybe you associate the villa with a sense of relaxation and comfort. Maybe you associate the money with security or respect. It is this emotional experience that drives you to go for the goal. If it is not there, then you are unlikely to achieve the goal. Refer to Figure 7.1 to see how you can break your goals down into their tangible and intangible aspects. This will help you be much clearer about what you want to achieve and why you want to achieve it.

GOAL

TANGIBLE MOTIVATORS	INTANGIBLE MOTIVATORS
• What do you want? • When do you want it? • How much do you want? • Who do you want to help you? • S.M.A.R.T.	• Why do you want it? • What *experience* do you want to create? • Imagine you have already achieved it. How do you now feel?

Figure 7.1 Breaking Goals into Tangible and Intangible Motivators

COMMITMENT AND EMOTIONAL CONNECTION

Commitment does not live exclusively in the domain of the Mental State Pillar. Commitment requires an emotional connection to your goal. Simply recognising that the goal is a good idea or logically necessary will only take you so far. So much time and energy are wasted by people working on goals to which they really have very little emotional connection. They are working on these goals because they think they "have to" or because they think they "should" or because their mother, father, husband, wife, etc. wants them to. Emotional connection is the key ingredient.

I used to work in marketing and marketing departments the world over know this fact very well. They rarely sell you the tangible product. Instead, they sell you the emotional experience *associated with* that product. Soap powder is a perfect example. It is not an exciting product and so the marketing department does not sell you the (tangible) soap powder itself. Instead, it sells you the (intangible) idea that "when you buy our soap powder, your kids will think you are a great parent". People might not want to pay much money for detergent, but they will pay a lot more for the feeling that comes with being seen as a great parent. It is a similar story with body sprays and perfumes: in reality, they are simply chemicals in a can or a bottle. So, rather than sell you the tangible product, the marketing department sells you the intangible feeling of being irresistible to the opposite sex. People will pay a lot of money for the feeling of desirability!

INTANGIBLE AND TANGIBLE MOTIVATORS

The sting in the tail is that, in reality, there is *no* link between the intangible and the tangible elements. Bummer! How do we know that? It is perfectly possible to have the sports car and not feel sexy, to have the villa and not feel relaxed or even to have the money and not feel secure—indeed, some of the richest people I know are the most *insecure*! Even if you *do* experience the emotional feeling that you were driven by, we have all had the experience of feeling so thrilled to own the latest phone model and then feeling all let down the next day, because the manufacturer has just introduced a new model. The link between the intangible and tangible is fleeting at best.

We shall return to this theme later on in the book but for now, just notice that even though you often know that, in reality the product you are buying will not provide the emotional experience you seek, you still buy it anyway! It looks like 21st-century human beings are not the supremely rational automatons that they pretend (and often aspire) to be! So, what do you do?

The key thing is to choose goals that you feel genuinely emotionally motivated by, while at the same time being aware that the achievement of the goal in and of itself is no guarantee of the emotional experience you are searching for.

Commitment also shows up in the domain of the Physical State Pillar: it is associated with certain postures. Stop for a moment and imagine the body posture of someone who is committed to their goal and then imagine the body posture of someone who is not committed. You will find that they are different.

When you align your Mental, Emotional and Physical State Pillars in such a way as to embody commitment, you give yourself the best possible opportunity to achieve your desired goal.

Ultimately the most powerful way to know what you are committed to in life is to look at your *results*. However, in order to let your results illuminate your commitment in this way, you must be willing to strip away all the excuses and stories about why you have what you have (and do not have) in your life. Remember the As Is/To Be & Intangible/Tangible Matrix in the previous chapter? We will explore this idea more closely in the next chapter when we look at responsibility.

TARGET SETTING

If you want to be effective at getting to where you say you want to go, then target setting is critical. If you just keep taking action and failing, it can eventually become dispiriting. One way to ease the pain of this process is to make a distinction between the overall goal, purpose or vision that you are chasing and what you will need to do to get there. These are two fundamentally different, albeit linked, things.

For example:

- If my purpose is to get married, then I will need to do certain things, such as going out and meeting new and eligible people.
- If my purpose is to gain muscle, then I will need to do certain things, such as resistance training or eating more calories.

Purpose Goals and Performance Targets

The purpose goal is different from the performance target. In practice, many people confuse these two things. They want to keep focussing on the purpose goal, but fail to commit to the necessary performance targets.

Performance targets are important to success because they are smaller, more short-term, specific and measurable than purpose goals. If you do them and do them successfully, over time you will eventually achieve your purpose goal. Of course, you need to select performance targets that, when achieved, really will take you closer to your purpose goal! Sometimes, you may require support from an expert in the relevant field in order to identify the best performance targets for your current situation.

Performance targets provide you with bite-sized goals that you can achieve, or not. They are still likely to be risks, but they are not the kind of risk that paralyses you with fear. Instead, they are risks that you believe you have a better-than-average chance of successfully completing, and they also provide you with real-time feedback on your progress towards your purpose goal.

Small, Short-Term Wins Build Confidence

If, especially early on in your journey, you are not hitting your performance targets, then you need smaller and/or shorter targets, because building your confidence is critical to your chances of achieving overall success.

A confident player is far more likely to achieve their goal and the one thing that builds confidence is success. Therefore, setting short, sharp performance targets that you believe you can either meet or exceed, is fundamental to achieving your purpose goal, especially in the early stages of your journey.[4]

For example, let's say my purpose goal is to get married. I might select the following performance targets for this week:

- Go on a date.
- Sign up with an online dating agency.
- Develop my capacity for openness by attending two group yoga sessions.
- Develop my capacity for vulnerability by speaking in public.

I see all these actions as "risks". They involve doing something different, they are specific and measurable, and at the end of the week, I know whether I have done them or not. Then, results in hand, I can debrief, ideally with a coach, going over my results, my lessons and my experience, and declare new performance targets for the following week, course-correcting as and when necessary.

---

4   I was first introduced to this method of working with confidence levels to support someone to win by Kelly Poulos, author of *Secrets to Winning.*

One of the most powerful aspects to discuss with your coach in this area is: while you were taking these risks, which domain did you experience the most/least discomfort in, the Physical, Mental or Emotional State Pillar? This conversation will provide very powerful information about your current habits and comfort zone. In turn, it will allow for a more informed discussion about how to choose appropriate performance targets for the following week.

As you begin to create success and your confidence grows, you can then set bigger performance targets over a longer time frame. However, if you do this too soon and you start failing to achieve the targets set, then that is feedback that you need to recalibrate and make the performance targets smaller and more short-term. Results are the ultimate feedback and if you let them be your coach with regard to the performance targets you set, then you have a far better chance of achieving your purpose goals.

08

WHAT STOPS ME GETTING THERE?

Start this section by reflecting on goals that you have not yet achieved but are still working on. If you are like most people, then you have many factors that exist outside of you: "I don't have enough time"; "I don't have enough money"; "my boss does not like me"; "my wife/husband is not supportive", etc. Or maybe you have a lot of internal factors that don't really stand up under scrutiny: "I am too old", "too young", "too tall", "too short", etc. Remember the section on assessments: such statements are not true or false, however much evidence you may have to support them!

What most people do not realise is that they are holding themselves back from achieving their goals for very practical reasons!

BARRIERS AND ENABLERS

If you achieve your goal, is it all good news? Conversely, if you do not achieve your goal, is it all bad news? Look at the Sarius Squares (Figure 8.1) to see what you might be missing:

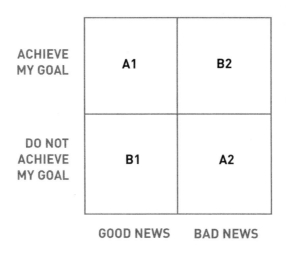

Figure 8.1 The Sarius Squares

Everyone likes to focus on the A squares: the good news if I do achieve my goal, and the bad news if I do not achieve my goal. These are the obvious, common things to look at, but the real power lies in the B squares: the good news if I do not achieve my goal and the bad news if I do achieve my goal. I know it sounds a little weird at first, but think about it a moment longer.

Let's take a couple of examples:

I want to get promoted at work:

A1: Good news if I achieve it: more money and an office of my own.

A2: Bad news if I do not achieve it: same old, same old, working for the same boss for another year.

Looks good, right? But wait…

B1: Good news if I do not achieve it: I can carry on coasting.

B2: Bad news if I do achieve it: More hours in the office and more performance evaluations to write at the end of the year.

I want to get married:

A1: Good news if I achieve it: steady relationship and no more dating.

A2: Bad news if I do not achieve it: my parents continue to be on my case!

But…

B1: Good news if I do not achieve it: I keep my independence and I can continue to look for Mister/Miss Perfect.

B2: Bad news if I do achieve it: I might make a mistake and meet the "right" person straight after the wedding.

So, feed your goal into this blank matrix (Figure 8.2) and see what pops up this time. Most likely, you will see a very different picture!

Figure 8.2 The Sarius Squares Exercise

One of the most useful personal development presuppositions that I use with my coaching clients is to start from a place where we assume that all the results they have in their life are the ones that they intended to have. (How did you do with *that* "O"?) Whether that is really true or not, it is the most powerful place to stand if you are serious about producing the goals you say you want in your life!

SELECTIVE RESPONSIBILITY

What most people like to do however is to be "selectively responsible". When they produce a result they *like*, they say: "I created that. It was my intention." When they produce a result they do *not* like, they say: "I did not create that. It was not my intention." I recently caught myself in this trap with regard to my fitness regime, when I noticed myself thinking this:

> *"My shirt feels tight: I have put on muscle from working out at the gym.*
> *My belt feels tight: that idiot dry cleaner shrunk my trousers."*

How very convenient! As soon as I produce a result that I am unhappy with, I find someone or something to blame. Remember, as we saw when we looked at honesty in Chapter 6, blaming *yourself* is also a trap. The problem is that I am now stuck. If I did not create that result, then I am at the mercy of other forces. I have to wait for the circumstances or other people to change before I can make progress. If I have been blaming myself, then in order to get unstuck, I have to be willing to admit that my self-accusation (eg. "I am too old") is simply an assessment rather than an assertion, and as such can be changed whenever I wish.

"Selective responsibility" is a trap: it keeps you stuck inside your (very reasonable) stories and explanations. Responsibility is like pregnancy. You are either pregnant or not pregnant. You are either responsible or not responsible.

Responsibility

The unwillingness to take responsibility for the current state of affairs is another very common factor that stops people achieving their goals. If you are unwilling to take responsibility for the present, then it is very unlikely that you see yourself as having the ability to produce the desired result in the future.

What seems to get in the way is a belief that if you take responsibility for the current state of affairs, then it means you are somehow to blame, wrong, bad, or at fault somehow. However, this does not follow at all; it is perfectly possible to acknowledge that you caused or created the current situation without seeing yourself at fault or to blame. In fact, a willingness to acknowledge your *input* into the situation is very freeing and leaves you with a sense of power. Imagine your life is a car: if you took the car *off* track in the past, then you can bring the car back *on* track in the future. The alternative is to be a backseat driver: always right, but ultimately powerless to move the car. To be clear, doing nothing also counts as input!

PERSONAL REFLECTION

Marcus: Responsibility

This was something that showed up very powerfully for me, early on in my own journey of self-discovery. When I was three years old, my parents divorced. This was, and always will be, a result in my life.

For many years, I oscillated between blaming myself and blaming my parents and, at some level, it "worked" for me: I used it as a great excuse for immature behavior and average results ("What can you expect? I am from a broken home"). It became a wonderful justification for all the nonsense I got myself into.

But then, when I was willing to look honestly and responsibly at my life, I realised that I had concocted this version of events as a convenient shield. My input or responsibility was not what I had done or had not done at the time (I was three years old!) but was everything to do with the *interpretation* and *attitude* that I was continuing to adopt with regard to the event, all those years later. This realisation was a slap in the face, but it was one that woke me up.

I shifted from "I'm from a broken home—poor me" to "I've got two dads, you've only got one?—poor you". These are two totally different assessments, based on the exact same assertion (my parents divorced when I was three). In that moment, I realised something immensely powerful that I have continued to bring forward in my life and that today informs all my coaching:

It is all made up.

I have compassion for myself and the *people* in my life but that compassion does not extend to my or their *stories*. The moment as a coach or as a leader that I buy into other people's stories, I am doomed. The moment I buy into my own story, I am stuck.

We do not create random interpretations and make up just any stories. Instead, the stories we make up serve a purpose. In my example, it served as a justification for average results and as a way to elicit sympathy, but it also kept me stuck.

09

IMAGE

The fear of seeing yourself (or being seen by others) as somehow bad or wrong shows up in other ways too. Let's look at one of the commonest issues that crops up in my coaching in the corporate world: "work/life balance". First of all, that is a horrible way to frame the issue, because it sets the client up for failure right from the start. The attempt to find a "balance" is doomed. What are you trying to balance? You have *one* life and part of that life is work. There is nothing to balance.

What people generally mean by "work/life balance" is really spending more time at home with the family, or more time on themselves, or in summary, what they *want* to do, rather than what they think they *have* to do. (On rare occasions, people have wanted to free up more time for work, but in my experience, these clients are a little scarcer!)

The problem with this issue, as is often the case, lies in how it is framed in the first place. Talking about work/life balance implies that there are only two things in the equation (work and life) and that a balance must be sought between them. However, this is not the case. In fact there are *three* elements to this problem and you can uncover the third by asking this question:

> *"If I told you that, next week, on Friday evening, I will give you $5 million, only if you handled all your work for the week responsibly* and *got home on time to be with the kids (or do whatever else it is that you tell yourself work is stopping you from doing), then do you think you would get it done?"*

If your answer to that question is "no", then double the amount to $10 million; that usually does the trick! Yes! You could do it under those conditions, but to achieve it, you would have to address the third element that lies buried under the apparent work/life dichotomy. The third element is your image or public identity. In order to achieve this and receive the $5 million, your image would take some knocks. For example, you might need to say "no" to your boss's requests or ask for support from a team member.

The hard truth is that you are willing to let that happen for $5 million, but not for the sake of your family. Is it possible to have a great family life and a great career? Yes, it is! Indeed many people on the planet do have both. However, if you notice that *you* do not have both, then that is something worth investigating. In this case, what your results are telling you is that you cannot have:

Great family life
Great career
and
Your image

Let's look at how this plays out.

THE SUPERHERO & THE NICE GUY/GAL

The two most common images that get in the way in this area are "Superhero" (which can easily morph into its close relative, "Control Freak") and "Nice Guy/ Gal".

The Superhero ends up spending more and more time in the office, in a desperate (and ultimately fruitless) attempt to prove (to themselves and others) that they indispensable, indestructible, omnipotent and omniscient. The Nice Guy/Gal ends up spending more and more time in the office in a desperate (and ultimately fruitless) attempt to have everyone like or respect them.

Interestingly, although the images are very different in one respect at least, they result in the same thing—an unwillingness to say "no" to people. However, by being unwilling to say "no" in the office, they end up saying "no" to their family (and/or themselves). The most common beliefs that drive people are:

"If I say no, people will think I cannot cope."
(hurts my image of omnipotence)

"If I say no, people will think I do not know how to do it."
(hurts my image of omniscience)

"If I say no, people will think I am not a nice person."
(hurts my image of "goodness")

"If I say no, people will lose respect for me."
(hurts my image of importance)

Net result: they end up choosing to prioritise their image and their career over their family. The whole "work/life balance" story is a smokescreen. The real issue is that the client wants to protect their *image*. So, to be clear:

Work/life balance is a myth.
There is simply life and how you choose to live it.

Your image has consequences across all Five Pillars of Performance. For example, consider how the physical state and posture of someone with a "superhero" image is going to be very different from someone with a "nice guy/gal" image. Similarly, their emotional state will be characterised by very different beliefs about which emotions are and are not acceptable to exhibit. Also, consider how your image affects the External Pillars of Support and Practice as well: Are you willing to ask for or accept support? Are you willing to practise?

FEAR OF FAILURE

Another very common area where "image protection" gets in the way of producing the result you say you want is the fear of failure. I have heard clients talk about this one almost as often as "work/life balance"! However, as with "work/life balance", the fear of failure is a total mirage, smoke and mirrors designed to obscure the real issue from view.

Do you think you have a fear of failure? If you do, then read on, because I am going to guess that you really don't and that something else is going on. Figure 9.1 can help illuminate the real issue.

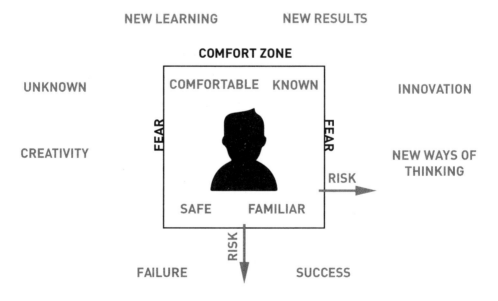

Figure 9.1 The Comfort Zone

Inside your comfort zone exist all the results that you already have and the results that you could achieve, if you chose to, without taking a risk. There are, however, other results that you say you want that exist outside your comfort zone. These are the results that you would need to take a risk to achieve.

The first thing to notice is that these results never miraculously show up inside your comfort zone of their own accord—*you* need to make them happen, and you make them happen by taking a risk.

As an example, and leading on from the work/life balance discussion above: let's say the goal you want to achieve is to spend more time with the family during the week. However, in order to achieve that, you need to take the risk of beginning to delegate. No one is going to give you that result, *you* need to make it happen.

What you tell yourself is, "I cannot do it because it will not work and I do not want to fail." However, look again at the diagram and you see that that logic does not add up. By not taking a risk, you are *guaranteeing* failure! When you don't take a risk, you stay in your comfort zone and that is the one place on the diagram where the new result will never show up! So, if you really *did* have a fear of failure, then you would be taking risks all the time! Something else is going on.

Once again it is your image that has you tied up in knots. What your image wants you to believe is this:

"If you fail, then you are a failure."

However, that's just not the case. If it were true, then Steve Jobs would be a failure because he got fired from Apple, Roger Federer would be a failure because he has lost in 10 Grand Slam finals, and Thomas Edison would be a massive failure because it took him 1,000 failures before he invented the light bulb!

The truth is that successful people fail way more often than unsuccessful people.

So, you are not really afraid of *failure*. Instead, you are afraid of being *judged as a failure* by others (and/or yourself). You are more interested in protecting your image than you are in creating the results that you say you want. More than that, if you think you are avoiding people's judgements by staying safe and hiding out in your comfort zone, then you are kidding yourself! Human beings are judgement machines and you will be judged just as much for playing safe as you will be for taking a risk. The only difference is that taking a risk carries with it the possibility of creating a new result in your life, whereas playing safe will keep you stuck with your current results.

I very often encounter this fear of failure when I am coaching middle and senior managers. They have done well in their careers and then suddenly they stop and look around. Suddenly they realise that they now have something to lose and so they start playing safe, waiting and holding back.

CLIENT CASE STUDY

Jeroen van Weesep, VP of Supply Chain at Lego, working with Marcus

Jeroen very successful by most standards: in his early 40s, he was a senior manager in a large multinational company. However, he had sought out a coach because of this nagging assessment that he was "no longer achieving all that he could". His learning curve was beginning to flatten out. He was facing a challenge that many successful people face. His comfort zone was very large and it was producing very good results. So, why change anything? Why risk stepping outside his comfort zone when his life was "OK"?

I discovered that when Jeroen reached that important milestone in his life of becoming senior manager, he unconsciously started to play safe and stopped taking risks to protect what he had achieved. He had begun to want to keep the high pace of achievement and learning while staying safe and comfortable in his comfort zone. That wasn't going to happen for him (and it isn't going to happen for you either).

Together, we identified the beliefs that formed the boundaries of Jeroen's comfort zone and began to gently loosen their grip on his actions.

As he developed the confidence to risk stepping outside his comfort zone, so his learning curve steepened again. The greater challenges came with a stronger sense of achievement for Jeroen, who has since realised that he needs to constantly challenge himself in order to maintain his progress.

If you have ever taken part in a ropes course or climbed a high ladder, you will have experienced the same phenomenon. While you are climbing up and focussing on the end goal, you are exhilarated, but when you stop climbing and look down to see how far up you have come, the fear kicks in and you cling on for dear life. The longer you stay stuck, the bigger the fear gets. The only way around this is to keep moving.

PERSONAL REFLECTION

Marcus: Fear of Failure

I well remember when I first encountered this idea. I was in my early 20s and having a tennis lesson with a coach when she asked me why I was having tennis lessons. At the time, I thought it was a weird question and I didn't even give my answer a second thought. I blurted out: "Because I want to win!" She looked at me and said: "Oh that's easy, I'll just have you play in the under 5's class all day!" Damnit.

In that moment, I realised that while winning is very nice and all, it was winning *challenging* games that was the key for me: games where there was a possibility of me losing. In order for that to happen, I had to be willing to play those games in the first place, and not just play them, but play them with every ounce of my soul.

So many people that I coach will only participate 100% when they know (or are pretty damn sure) that they will win. They usually hold something back, very often with the internal logic that "if I lose this game, I can always say to myself (and others) that I didn't go 100%, and if I *had* tried 100%, then I would most likely have won!" This kind of logic is a great way to protect your image, but it is also a great way to ensure that you never experience peak performance and win the big ones, the ones that you really want to win!

It is the process of risking failure that expands your comfort zone. The first time I spoke in public was a terrifying experience, but now, many years later, speaking in public is how I earn my living!

Many clients I work with have an internal conversation that sounds like this: "*When* I feel confident, *then* I'll take that risk." What they fail to realise is that life actually happens the other way around: "*After* I take the risk, *then* I feel confident." Unfortunately, this means that they never do feel confident because they just never take that risk!

You can spend your life holding back, playing safe, protecting your image and die a little every day, or you can step out into life, take risks and recreate your life in every moment. The choice is yours.

10

MOODS

The final element that I want to highlight that stops someone from getting what they want concerns the Emotional State Pillar and in particular, the prevailing mood in which they live their life. Moods act as predispositions for action; they set the context for possibility.[5] For example, if you wake up in the morning in a mood of joy and excitement, then pretty much anything seems possible. However, if you wake up in a mood of depression and frustration, then pretty much everything seems impossible. It is the same world; only your mood has changed.

---

5   I first became aware of the importance of moods in the NFA coaching program
     and the book *A General Theory of Love* by Thomas Lewis, Fari Amini and
     Richard Lannon.

For the purpose of this section, I shall define an emotion as a feeling that occurs as a result of your assessment of a situation or event, while a mood is a feeling that exists independent of any one event. Instead, it operates like software running in the background of your computer: you cannot see it, but it is there all the time.

Learning to work with moods (your own and other people's) is a key area to investigate if you want to create peak performance for yourself or to lead others effectively. As a human being, you are always living in a mood. Teams have moods, families have moods, cities have moods, countries have moods. There is no way out of that. The question is: what mood are you living in?

WHAT CREATES MOODS?

The prevailing mood in which you are living is created or influenced by various factors: your emotional state, your physical state and your mental state.

First, your emotional state: the mood in which you grew up as a child and the mood you surround yourself with today. Moods are created and sustained by immersion within specific feelings and emotions. The longer you are exposed to a certain mood, the stronger that mood becomes in you. A good analogy is brewing tea: the longer you leave the teabag in the pot, the stronger the tea becomes. The longer you live in a mood of resentment, the stronger that mood becomes in you. For example, a child who grows up surrounded by a mood of anger tends to grow up living in either a mood of anger or fear and that mood then becomes invisible to them: "situation normal". A manager who works in a team where trust is low for a sustained period of time will begin to experience a mood of distrust. Similarly, you can also develop a certain mood if you consistently experience the same emotional response to events. In the end, the emotion remains after the events have ended, and the short-term emotional response becomes a long-term mood.

Next, your physical state: the mood in which you live is connected to your body. Only certain moods can live in certain bodies. If you tend to slouch, round your shoulders and look to the floor as you walk, then it is very difficult to experience real joy. Conversely, if you walk with your head held high and your shoulders thrown back, and you establish eye contact with those around you, then it is very difficult to experience real sadness. Your mood influences your body and your body influences your mood: your emotional and physical states are interrelated.

Finally, your mental state: the assessments you make about yourself, other people and the world as a whole also influence your mood. For example, once you form the assessment that "people cannot be trusted", then moods of fear and anxiety become very common. How you see something determines how you feel, and, how you feel determines how you see it. Conversely, once the feeling of fear becomes a habit, then it is easy to form the assessment that "people cannot be trusted". In this way, your emotional and mental states are also interrelated.

WHAT SHIFTS MOODS?

If you aspire to become a leader, then learning to identify, name and work with moods is imperative because of how they set limits on what is seen as possible in any situation. A team with a mood of resignation is highly unlikely to achieve great results.

The factors that generate moods also shed light on how to shift them (both your own moods and the moods of those around you). What does not work is to simply *instruct* yourself or someone else to change their mood. Moods do not respond to instruction. Consider what happens when someone tells you to relax. On hearing this instruction, most people do exactly the opposite: they tense up! They start to think, "Why do I need to relax? Why is he telling me to relax? What is the looming danger that I need to worry about?", and end up winding themselves up even further.

Rather than instruction, your emotional state responds to the same three factors that create moods: your emotional state, your physical state and your mental state.

With regard to your Emotional State Pillar, you can shift your mood by developing practices that put you in positions and places where you can *experience* the mood you desire. For example, if you notice that you are stuck in a mood of sadness, then developing a regular practice of watching stand-up comedy shows or funny YouTube videos will have an impact on your mood.

To shift your mood via your Physical State Pillar, practise moving your body out of its habitual shapes and patterns. One of the quickest ways to begin shifting a negative mood is to get your body moving in different ways and at different speeds. Adopting a regular practice of movement, such as dancing, boxing or some other physical activity can greatly impact your mood.

Shifting your mood via your Mental State Pillar entails being willing to look closely at how you see things and to realise that the way you see the world is not the way it is; it is just the way you see the world. Once you remember that "it is all made up", you will be able to make different assessments and therefore choices about how to see the situation and how to act in that situation. These new assessments, choices and actions can help to shift your mood.

It can be very freeing to realise that you can shift your mood, because it means that you don't have to be stuck in any mood if you don't wish to be.

THE WAY YOU SEE IT IS NOT THE WAY IT IS

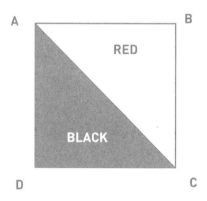

A   sees red to the left, black to the right
B   sees only red
C   sees black to the left, red to the right
D   sees only black

Figure 10.1 Viewing Point Determines Point of View

Figure 10.1 illustrates the point perfectly. There is one square, but how you see it depends entirely on where you stand; your point of view depends entirely on your viewing point. For example, if you stand at corner B then you will swear the world is red but if you stand at corner D then you will swear the world is black. If you stand at corner A, you will see red to the left of you and black to the right of you, whereas someone standing at point C will see it in reverse.

In other words, your assessments are not assertions, and so for example, as long as you see the world as being out to get you, you can expect to live in a mood of distrust or a mood of fear. If you are willing to shift your assessment, then you can shift your mood. In the above diagram this is represented by being willing to move from one vantage point to another in order to see what others see. This is often called "standing in someone else's shoes" and it is why the old adage advises us not to judge someone until we have walked a mile in their shoes. The world can look very different depending on where you see it from, and where you see it from has a major bearing on your assessments, which in turn go a long way in creating your mood.

If for example, you are standing at point B in the diagram where you can only see red and someone standing at point D starts talking about seeing black, and you are unwilling to shift your perspective or viewing point, then it will be very easy for you to become frustrated and angry. You might want to scream: "What is this 'black' that you are talking about? All I can see is red!" Once you are stuck in anger, then it can easily become infectious and suddenly, the person at point D also becomes angry and a full-blown argument ensues. The longer the argument goes on, the more fixed the two parties (individuals, departments, companies or countries!) become, and the less hope there is of one or both of them being willing to uproot their viewing point and move to a different one.

When you are angry and trapped in an argument like this, very often you will eventually say something that you end up regretting. This is because you trigger your fight-or-flight mechanism: your breath becomes shallow and your body starts to shift the flow of blood away from your neocortex and towards your muscles, so that you are ready to defend yourself physically or run away from the danger. With blood flowing away from your neocortex, you are less likely to make sound choices at this point. Yes—the angrier you become, the stupider you become!

In contrast, if the person standing at point B is willing to stand at point D (or vice versa), even if just for a moment or two, then there is at least the possibility of *understanding*, if not a full reconciliation between the two viewpoints. However, if the person at point B is in a prevailing mood of anger or impatience then the likelihood of this movement happening is remote. Imagine however, if the person standing at point B has a prevailing mood of enthusiasm or curiosity: in this case, it is far more likely that they would be willing to stand at point D and explore the situation from a different vantage point. This is why moods are so important; they create the framework for what someone sees as possible in a situation. They are a disposition for action.

**PART I:
SELF-REFLECTION**

Here's a chance to put down your "X" filters and honestly answer the questions posed in these sections, so that you give yourself the best possible chance of creating a new path.

WHO AM I?
Assessments and Assertions

Pay attention to the distinction between assertions and assessments to note down what you have decided about yourself:

1. I assert that I am:

2. I assess that I am:

Be careful! This is a tricky exercise. For example, the statement "I like football" is an *assessment*, not an assertion. Why? Because your standards of "liking" may be very different to mine, therefore it is not *true* or *false* to say: "I like football". All that statement does is to highlight your standards of "liking".

Look closely at whatever you have written in your list of assessments, because without any intervention or change, these are likely to be highly predictive of your future!

As shown in Chapter 5, the following exercise gets you thinking about how an assertion about yourself can generate many assessments as well. Use one of the assertions you have written in the previous exercise to see what assessments you have tacked on to it:

Assertion: I am _____.

Because I am _____,

I can _____.
I cannot _____.

I must _____.
I must not _____.

Other people must _____.
Other people must not _____.

I need to _____.
I don't need to _____.

_____ are _____.
_____ are not _____.

Remember that if you are willing to do this exercise honestly, it will not only make sense of much of your past and explain much of your present, but it will also be highly predictive of your future.

WHERE AM I?
Honesty

Take a moment and see if you can get clear on where you really are in your life, compared to where you are pretending to be. This one can be very difficult to do on your own: your own reasons and excuses have become so familiar to you, that they often become transparent and "situation normal". Maybe this is the time to enlist some support?

With someone you trust, note down what your results tell you about where you *really* are:

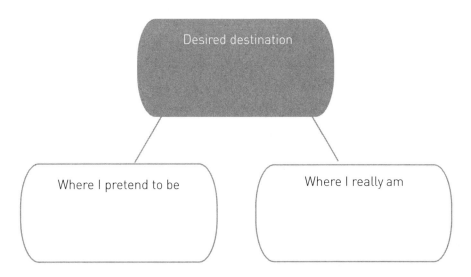

In order to do this you have to be willing to focus squarely on your results and avoid even a hint of explanation, justification or rationalisation. Remember, by telling the truth about where you are right now, you are not blaming yourself or admitting to being a bad person in any way. You are just being honest with yourself about how your input has created your situation.

WHERE AM I?
Entitlement

It can be difficult to identify your own areas of entitlement, but see if you can note down areas of your life where you see yourself as "entitled" or "un-entitled". People rarely like to admit this, but one way to access the areas where this is showing up is again to look at your results. Areas where you are stuck and not achieving the results you say you want are prime candidates to investigate!

1. Areas where I feel "entitled":

2. What I think I am entitled to do/not do in those areas:

3. Areas where I feel "un-entitled" or "un-deserving":

4. What I think I am not entitled to do/not do in those areas:

WHERE DO I WANT TO GO?
Goals and Emotional Connection

What you are currently working on and why do you want it?

1. My current goal is:

2. Why I want it:

Now take a moment to set down some goals you are considering to work on in the future.

3. My future goal is:

4. Why I want it:

What do you notice about your answers? This is a good time to assess whether you are committed (physically, mentally and emotionally connected) to your current and future goals or whether you are just going through the motions and wasting your own time and very often the time of other people as well.

WHAT STOPS ME GETTING THERE?
It Is All Made Up

Consider three events in your life (past or present) where you are experiencing or have experienced frustration, resignation, anger or other separating emotion. For each event, answer the following questions: What story are you making up about it? How does that story serve you? Consider the input you had in the event turning out the way it did.

Be careful. This is not a "coulda, woulda, shoulda" session. Only note down what you actually did, didn't do and the attitude you are choosing to take with regard to that particular event. How can you create a different, more empowering version of events? Remember: it is all made up!

1.

2.

3.

Image and Fear of Failure

Take a moment here to consider what you have discovered about your image and how you see failure. These are very powerful factors to become aware of.

1. The image I present to others:

2. What I have been doing to present such an image:

3. What I am afraid people will see if I drop my image:

4. Areas of my life where I have been telling myself I have a fear of failure:

MOODS

1. The prevailing mood or moods that operate in my life:

2. Given the mood(s) I have identified, the implications for the possibilities that are or are not open to me:

3. How I can shift any limiting moods that I have identified:
    (Consider practices in your mental, emotional and physical states.)

PERSONAL DEVELOPMENT AND THE FIVE PILLARS OF PERFORMANCE

There were some big "O's" in this section. Pay attention to how you fared maintaining your openness to them!

Before you move on to Part II, take a moment to note down what you have noticed about yourself with regards to each of the Five Pillars of Performance:

What I have discovered about myself in Part I:

1. Mental State Pillar – My beliefs about myself, other people, and the world are: (Pay particular attention to the beliefs that you see limiting your effectiveness.)

2. Emotional State Pillar – The moods and emotions I am accustomed to experiencing and the ones I am not accustomed to experiencing are:

3. Physical State Pillar – What I notice about my body, my posture and the physical sensations I experience is:

4. Practice Pillar – What I repeatedly do; the practices I have adopted (consciously or unconsciously) are:

5. Support Pillar – The areas where I am asking for support, and the areas where I am not asking for support; the people I am asking for support from, and the people I am not asking for support from:

And finally…

The three most powerful things I have noticed about myself and my life so far while reading Part I of this book are:

1.

2.

3.

Look back over your answers in this self-reflection and consider the implications they have over your life as you move forward.

FROM PERSONAL DEVELOPMENT TO THE BODY

This completes the first part of your journey. In it I have sought to illustrate some of the fundamental building blocks of personal development that I use in my coaching and leadership development work.

You will have noticed that, in most instances in this section, although we began with questions dealing with the Mental State Pillar, it was never long before the Emotional and Physical State Pillars cropped up. This demonstrates how important it is to consider yourself and those around you in totality, rather than to artificially split out or prioritise one of the states or pillars.

Indeed, if you want to make shifts in one pillar, then very often the shift is most effectively made by addressing one of the other two pillars. For example, making a shift in the Physical State Pillar is often the most powerful way to intervene in the Emotional State Pillar. Moods and emotions live in and are associated with certain postures. If you are willing to move or hold your body in a different way, then you can begin to open up the possibility of experiencing different emotions and moods.

In the second part of your journey, Sari will take over and she will introduce you to your body and the critical role it can play in helping you create peak performance for yourself and the people you aspire to lead. This is the piece of the jigsaw puzzle that so many people downplay or even ignore altogether. However, although we are now about to focus on the Physical State Pillar, you will again see the integrated nature of all the pillars and how the Mental and Emotional State Pillars influence and are influenced by the Physical State Pillar.

Only when we have explored the world of personal development *and* the body can we move onto the final destination of this book: a transformative approach towards leadership that encompasses both self-awareness *and* physical movement.

Buckle up for Part II. Here comes Sari.

PART II

THE BODY

BY SARI

(CHAPTERS 18 TO 21 BY MARCUS)

11

THE TRANSPARENT BODY

Whatever we do and wherever we do it, we are taking action through our physical bodies. To evoke general body awareness in my personal training clients, my favourite coaching questions include:

- How do you treat your body?
- What would happen if you treated your business/career the same way as you treat your body?
- Simply by standing or walking, what message are you sending to the world?
- How open are you to receiving non-verbal messages from others?
- Can you sense leadership presence in other people?

These questions often have my clients stop in their tracks, because they have not really considered such questions before. They are expecting a "normal" personal trainer who will just focus on weights and reps.

Becoming conscious of your Physical State Pillar very often results in a trip back in time, to a time when your physical habits began to take shape.

PERSONAL REFLECTION

Sari: The Transparent Body

People cannot read your mind and they cannot feel your heart but even before they get to know you, what they can see is your physical body. I well remember many occasions as a child when I spoke my mind and what happened next. One time, I tasted my neighbour's cookie, put it back on the plate and said, "It is not a nice cookie." My mother stared at me hard, physically signalling that what I did was not acceptable, and I understood her even though she did not say a word. Looking into her eyes made me feel intensely uncomfortable, both physically and emotionally. I began to calculate what I needed to say and do in order to gain a different physical reaction from my mother.

As I grew older, I learned to associate raising my hand to speak with an increase in my heartbeat. Conversely, if I kept my hand down, choosing not to speak up, I would experience a strong "chemical reaction" inside my body, an experience I learned to connect to an assessment of self-criticism and disappointment with myself. When I did speak up, I noticed a shaky voice and a shaky body: I was afraid of being judged again. But what people actually saw was a tight, shaking body; what they heard was a shaky voice.

Now, imagine this physical experience being repeated over and over again, without any intervention. In the end this physical experience just became "situation normal", the shakiness, tightness and rigidity existed regardless of whether I was about to speak up or not. I had embodied it through unthinking repetition. We grow up in a society full of expectations and we use the body as the easiest way to hide or suppress what we do not want the world to see in us: "You cannot cry if you want to be seen as a 'big girl'."

In my coaching, I encounter similar examples every day, where physical patterns, learned a long time ago, show up in the way that people hold themselves many years later. The end result is often a lack of authenticity, with emotions and thoughts struggling to emerge from a body that simply will not let them out. It is as though people live in an invisible physical prison of their own making.

I often ask clients the following questions:

- What if you were to show up authentically, so that what we see in you physically were to accurately reflect what you are thinking and feeling?
- What if your walk were to actually match your talk?
- What would happen if you were that transparent?
- What kind of leadership would you then be embodying?

In this way, I begin to work with my clients on all three of the Internal Pillars of Performance: looking to create alignment between Physical, Emotional and Mental State Pillars. There is a lot more to your Physical State Pillar than simply weights and cardio!

MOVEMENT, FITNESS AND LEADERSHIP

One of the developments in leadership over the last few years has been the desire to be seen as "authentic" and to create "leadership presence". Authenticity involves bringing together all three of the Internal Pillars of Performance in an aligned or congruent manner and requires leaders to be *physically visible* as well as transparent in feeling and thought. Very often the missing ingredient is body awareness.

Leadership presence involves being seen, being vulnerable, being exposed and engaging with people physically, emotionally and mentally such that they are encouraged to do the same with others. If you want to engage with people at this deep a level, then paying attention to your body is no longer just a nice thing to do, it is an imperative. You cannot hide your physicality any more. The message in this part of the book is to look at your physical body as a place to create who you want to be now and in the future, rather than as a place to reflect who you have been in the past.

> *"A strong leader actually affects the environment around them without even saying anything. This is because they have an expansive leadership presence."*
> - Wendy Palmer, founder of Leadership Embodiment

I have long been fascinated by leadership presence. How is it that some people are able to influence people with little verbal communication while others struggle to make a similar impact? Can we actually develop leadership qualities using fitness movements? I believe we can, and we will go into more depth on this in Part III.

Working in both disciplines—leadership and fitness—with a wide range of clients, I started paying attention to their posture and their gestures. It did not take long for me to see how a shift in posture can create a shift in how a person thinks, feels and speaks, and therefore in how able they are to engage with and lead others.

My quest led me to join a fitness physique competition—where there are no words and it is only your walk and posture that communicates with the audience and the judges. I watched how some competitors would walk on the stage and create a powerful impact and how other, similarly muscled participants would create a much weaker impact. For some, their beautifully developed body (their Physical State Pillar) was simply not enough for them to engage powerfully with the audience and judges because their Mental and Emotional State Pillars were communicating a very different story. Their "new" body was still communicating their old thoughts and feelings, developed long ago.

I began to experience a leadership that went beyond the eyes, the ears and the heart. The ability to engage people at a deeper level seemed to transcend this and required an alignment of thoughts, feelings and physicality. It was this experience that ultimately led me to develop the Five Pillars of Performance with Marcus; this system now forms the backbone of my coaching and this book.

PERSONAL REFLECTION

Sari: Movement, Fitness and Leadership

Being a champion in my fitness physique category I am often asked to coach athletes to pose and/or walk in a way that will engage the judges. A walk—how difficult it can be, right? As it turns out, when you seek to bring leadership presence into your walk, things are not quite as simple as they seem.

When coaching bodybuilders or fitness athletes about their walk, posture and pose, my first questions include:

- What do you want to create with your walk?
- What values do you want to embody?
- Why are you doing this?

These questions lead them to explore their core values. We need to start here: talking about what matters to them and what they are emotionally connected to in their purpose. I am working with them to build their leadership presence through body posture and movement. Something as simple as walking has a profound impact on how you set yourself up to engage with the people around you. Once they are in touch with their emotional connection to their purpose, their physical body can then communicate freely, and suddenly they can engage with people at a whole new level.

I recently coached a squad of domestic helpers from the Aidha school in Singapore. Their dream was simple: to dance competitively onstage in a powerful way. But I am a movement coach, not a dance coach! We chose simple movements, with a strong emphasis on who they wished to be when they danced: confident, worthy and strong women.

When we started, they all danced with what I term a "looking for coins on the floor" motion, not daring to make any physical connection with their audience. It does not matter how fancy the movements are; if you are not embodying your personal values, then the quality of your movement will be poor and your ability to engage with the audience will be minimal. This is just as true in the boardroom as it is on the dance floor. Therefore, my coaching focussed on who they were willing to be as they moved, rather than on the movement itself. What values were they willing to embody?

They eventually emerged the first runner-up in the competition, and even appeared in the national news. What made me proud is that although they were not the most technically gifted dancers in the competition, they projected their values as they moved. It was the resulting engagement with the audience and the judges that shone through and created stunning results. No more looking for coins!

As I have begun to work with more and more people in a business context, I see exactly the same phenomenon: the Physical State Pillar, once unshackled from its historical context and learned habits, can be the secret weapon that gives people the edge in their ability to engage powerfully with others and ultimately create the results of their dreams. This important aspect of personal growth, development and leadership is absolutely trainable via purposeful, conscious body-based interventions and practices.

12

FITNESS TODAY

Fitness today is not supposed to be easy or fun! Now you are working out, not just for the bedroom or the beach but to ensure your very survival. We have moved from "Happy Fit" to "Cross Fit" in every sense of the term. Much of fitness today revolves around pushing your physical limits. Marketing focuses on words such as "extreme", "boot camps" and "amped". Injury is seen as a badge of honour. If you do not get injured from time to time, then you are clearly not pushing hard enough!

It is in that moment of injury that the penny often drops for people: the injury has cost them their freedom of motion. As with so many areas of coaching, the awareness follows some kind of breakdown, where what was transparent is suddenly made visible. When you lose your freedom of motion you notice its importance very quickly.

Leaders who wake up to the importance of their Physical State Pillar in this era of "go hard or go home" are especially vulnerable in this regard. Armed with information from the internet, they stride into the gym ready to "hit it and hit it hard", but their lack of experiential learning in the workout world, combined with their desire to "win" and their unwillingness to engage support, leads to an unhappy end. I have seen this pattern repeated time and time again. The only winners are the physiotherapists.

There is not yet enough of a voice for those who want to be fit, while learning what it means to be an athlete and leader at the same time. What a big miss. Some can be great athletes and some can be great leaders—but few make the connection between what their body has learned during their physical training and the situation they are facing in the office and at home.

What should you do when everything seems mainstream and extreme at the same time? Where should you start?

DEFINING FITNESS

I will start with the concept of "fitness" because this is very often what people first think of when they consider their body. What does "fit" mean? There are many different definitions, but ultimately, it is *your* answer that matters, so consider what fitness means to you. How do you decide if you (or someone else) are fit or not fit? What standards do you apply to fitness? Maybe it is a specific, tangible standard: your body weight, ability to lift a certain weight or run a certain distance in a certain amount of time. Or maybe it is a more general intangible standard: feeling out of breath when you go up a flight of stairs or play with the kids.

Here's a standard dictionary definition of fitness:

"The quality of being suitable to fulfill a particular role or task."

In our context, therefore, the pertinent question is: "Are you fit to lead"? What does this question even mean? The question behind being fit to *lead* is: are you set up, mentally, physically and emotionally, to do this thing called "leadership" or to be this thing called a "leader"?

In the past, if you wanted to develop your "fitness" to be a leader, then the approach would focus on your mental or cognitive state: you would either read books or do an MBA where you would listen to people tell you about leadership, then read more books and write papers about what you remembered from lectures and reading. As set out in Part I, the approach outlined here is rather different. It is not meant to remove the cognitive approach entirely, but it will place the focus elsewhere.

In Part I of this book, Marcus looked at some key elements of personal development which tended to begin in the domains of the Mental or Emotional State Pillars. Here in Part II, I will focus more squarely on the Physical State Pillar and look not only at some benefits of working with your physical state, but also at some interesting parallels between physical training and leadership development. However, just as in Part I, you will quickly begin to see the tight integration of the three Internal Pillars of Performance. Then in Part III, Marcus and I will look more closely at leadership development, and synthesise a new approach that firmly establishes the role of the Physical State Pillar alongside the Mental and Emotional State Pillars.

The whole proposition of this book is that if you really want to maximise your growth, learning and development as a leader, then willingness to work with *all three* of the Internal Pillars of Performance is critical: Mental, Emotional *and* Physical. In fact, given that most people focus on the Mental and Emotional State Pillars, then it is your willingness to engage with your Physical State Pillar that will give you that edge over others.

I am not saying that you need to be a world-class athlete in order to be a world-class leader. However, what I am saying is that there are some elements of physical training, movement and nutrition that can absolutely support you in your desire to become a more effective leader than you are today.

PERSONAL REFLECTION

Marcus: Defining Fitness

I know from talking with hundreds of coaching clients over the years, that my personal journey is similar to many people who enter a corporate life. When I was a child, I played all sorts of sports and generally ran around like a mad thing, until I joined the corporate world. After that, there was a general slow-down in my activity level, until by my late 30s, I wasn't really doing very much physical activity at all.

In my mid-30s, I had left my marketing job at Unilever and joined the personal development, leadership development and coaching world. As a result, I had started doing even more travelling and was developing even better excuses for not keeping fit or eating healthily.

Then one day, I looked over some photos taken at a friend's wedding, and I didn't like what I saw. For the first time in my life, I looked overweight. I am 6 feet and 2 inches tall and so had been able to hide it for a while, but I had reached 95 kg, and it did not look so good on me.

I remember very clearly what I did next. I sat down and gave myself a choice: either carry on getting out of shape and be OK with it, or enjoy doing something about it. It was very clear that I was not going to entertain a third option: carry on getting out of shape and feel guilty about it. I chose the latter. It was time to do something about it. The best things I did were to sign up for a gym membership and personal training sessions with a PT whom I enjoyed training with. The benefits of this were two-fold: I had made a sizeable financial commitment that I didn't want to waste, and I had enlisted support from someone who knew about training, could keep me on track and keep me safe. Left to my own devices, I would have given up or hurt myself for sure.

Honestly, back then, I really had no idea about any of this fitness stuff, but I trusted the person I was training with and while I supplied the commitment, she supplied the knowledge. It proved to be a potent combination. Within six months, I'd dropped 18 kg down to 77 kg, going from a 36-inch to a 32-inch waist. This created a slightly different problem. I had gone too far and had become very thin! That was when I decided to learn more about nutrition, which became the final part of the jigsaw puzzle. Pretty quickly after I started learning about nutrition, my weight settled at about 85 kg and has hovered around that level ever since.

I remember that when I started out, I encountered a lot of skepticism and cynicism: "Oh, it will never last... you won't be able to keep it up." When you try and make a big change, you soon find out who is really on your team, and who has just been pretending! This was one of the hardest parts for me to deal with: for example, watching other people's reactions when I cracked out a peanut butter and tuna on rye sandwich at 11 am, in the middle of a meeting!

However, I soon learned that there was truth in the old adage "nothing succeeds like success". After a few months, the laughing and cynicism had disappeared and had been replaced by congratulations and people asking me for tips! I think everyone was hoping that I had discovered a secret pill or a one-minute exercise routine that helped me drop the weight. They all looked a little disappointed when I told them it was a simple combination of diet and exercise!

Fast forward 10 years and people congratulate me on my discipline and willpower, but what I tell them is that it is no longer about that. I now *enjoy* exercising and eating clean. It is no longer something that I need to work hard at. It has become part of my identity—"who I assess myself to be in the world"—and as we saw in Part I, when something becomes part of your identity, for better or worse, it becomes difficult to shift. Similarly, in Part I, we also saw that we become good at what we repeatedly do. I have practiced my nutrition and exercise habits for so long that they are now largely automatic, and so the need for discipline and willpower are no longer the big factors they were 10 years ago.

By the way, before we return to the main narrative, I should point out that I am no exercise and nutrition robot. I love chocolate and cake more than most other people out there, and am certainly not afraid to eat them! (See Appendix I for one of my favourite treats.)

There was one other factor in my story. As I began my journey to handle my nutrition and exercise, Sari, then my girlfriend, joined me in this journey, and as usual with Sari, she caught up to me and then left me in the dust, as she went on to become a personal trainer and, ultimately, a champion in fitness physique competitions across Southeast Asia. Sari is also now an ICF-credentialled coach and not only have we provided support for each other, we have also grown together. Indeed, this book is really the product of hundreds of conversations between the two of us, examining the world of personal development and leadership and the world of the body, exercise and nutrition and finding more and more links between the two worlds in the process. In the end, we decided that we had to write a book!

A BROADER DEFINITION

I am a certified personal trainer with the National Academy of Sports Medicine (NASM), and they define physical fitness as follows:

"The ability of an individual to perform the physical demands of daily activities."[6]

---

6   National Academy of Sports Medicine (NASM). *NASM Essentials of Personal Fitness Training*. Edited by Micheal A. Clark, Scott C. Lucett, and Brian G. Sutton. Lippincott Williams & Wilkins. 2011.

This is similar to the definition outlined at the start of the chapter, but now I want to add an extra dimension: namely that for me, being "fit" really means being able to take care of what matters to you and the people you care about.

Fitness is usually defined as being somewhat *internally* focussed, but for me it includes the element of being focussed *outwards*, being able to take care of the needs of the people around you in your life. Because of this, I have always seen "fitness" as a critical factor in relationships in general and leadership, in particular. In addition, properly understood, fitness involves the emotional and mental states as well as the physical state. Emotional fitness gives me the courage to change. Mental fitness enables me to shift my conversation from "I can't" to "I can".

I am especially passionate about working with women to help them create fitness in their life. And when I say "fitness", I mean it in the widest sense of the word: physical, mental and emotional. I meet so many women in my line of work who lack the courage to change (emotional), who believe that they can't change (mental) and who also lack the physical fitness to make that change happen. Expanding their definition of fitness to include the physical, mental and emotional elements has ignited a strong sense of ownership over their personal goals.

What I have observed in personal training these days is that trainers often overemphasise the word "training" at the expense of "personal". At the end of the day, personal training is about connecting to what really matters to that person as a whole, integrated human being.

13

LEARNING TO MOVE

Isn't your body just that inconvenient thing that carries your brain around? For a large number of people, maybe even the majority, this is still the truth. They only really pay attention to their body when it breaks down in some way. When that happens, they grudgingly do what is necessary to fix it before going back to the old habits that created the problem in the first place! At the simplest level of all, consider this fundamental truth:

If you don't have your health,
then everything else in your life is a struggle.

As you will see as we go forward, being healthy is only ground zero as far as your Physical State Pillar is concerned, but it is a place to start.

People know their health is important but they just take it for granted. Why? Because when they are in good health for a long time, it becomes transparent, and they stop noticing it. This is true of many things in life; you only become aware of oxygen when it is taken away. If you are sitting down to read this book, then you most likely will not think about the chair, unless it breaks and you fall off it! This transparency can work for or against you in your desire to develop new habits. While you are trying to develop a new habit, it makes things difficult and uncomfortable, because there is no sense of transparency with a new action. However, once you do establish a new habit, the transparency returns and you can forget about it; it will happen automatically. When you maintain it, then what started out as a "diet" simply becomes a "lifestyle".

LEARNING

Where in your body does learning occur? Most people automatically think of the brain, and that is certainly where a lot of *information* is stored. However, the question was about where *learning* occurs. The answer to that isn't quite so clear. Do we learn mentally? Yes. Do we learn emotionally? Yes. Do we learn physically? Yes!

- Are you told at an early age not to play in the traffic?
- Is your learning rather different if you watch someone you care about play in the traffic and get hurt?
- Is your learning different again if you play in the traffic yourself and get hurt?

In all three examples, you learn. In the first example, you learn mentally, in the second, you learn emotionally, and in the third, you learn physically. Which one do you think will stay with you the longest?

Human beings learn best by doing. Think of how you learned to drive a car, ride a bike or to speak a second language. You probably didn't rely on just reading a book. You got on the bike (literally or metaphorically) and rode, fell off, got up and rode again. Doing or acting requires you to involve your body in some way. When you do that, the learning will really stick.

Learning and Your Body

> *"Knowledge is only a rumour, until it lives in the muscle."*
> - Traditional Indonesian saying

Consider this definition of knowing:

> *"To know is to be able to perform effective action."*

When I have truly *learned* something, I can be said to *know* it, and when I know it, I am able to *do* it. There is a big distinction between "know-how" (the Mental State Pillar) and what I term "know-do" (the Physical State Pillar). In the 21st century, "know-how" comes pretty cheap, but the capacity to really "know-do" is at a premium, and many people like to confuse the two. "Know-how" is a purely mental state, and as such, is very comfortable to acquire: I can read a book or search Wikipedia and minutes later, without leaving my chair, I can attain "know-how". Centuries ago, that information might have been gold dust and a path to fame and fortune, but today, on its own, it really counts for very little.

Conversely, the acquisition of "know-do" requires you to get uncomfortable (it requires you to experience something different in the domain of your Emotional State Pillar): you have to actually *do* something, and if it is something new, then inherent in that doing is making mistakes, losing face, recognition, efficiency and/or relationships. For many people, the loss of even one of those four things is worse than dying!

Take a moment here to consider how this relates to your own life. In which areas are you confusing "know-how" with "know-do"?

"Know-how" does not necessarily lead to "know-do", but if you have developed "know-do" then "know-how" automatically comes with it. You might not have the "official" information or possess the "right" way to do it, but if you have the "know-do", then at the very least, you will have developed some form of personal "know-how".

So, at a very fundamental level, if you want to develop as a leader, or if you want to grow in *any* respect, then it will require you to put your body into the equation: you need to *do* something. If you are only willing to put your brain into the game, then you are hampering your ability to win the game right from the outset. If you want to put your body into the game, then you want it to be fit, functional and healthy when it actually enters the fray.

The willingness to have your body play a role in your learning and the willingness to keep it healthy are two major factors in how far and fast your development will go.

We live and learn in our whole body, not simply in our heads.

However, as we shall see later on, we have only just begun to scratch the surface. When you start to move, exercise and take care of your nutrition, you supercharge your development efforts!

MAKING EVERY MOVEMENT COUNT

> *"The human body is incapable of not practising."*
> - Richard Strozzi-Heckler, *The Leadership Dojo*

Being sedentary has become "normal". It is so much more comfortable to sit and watch others move around than to actually do it ourselves. When everything is so easily accessible at the click of a button, why bother moving at all? Many people's jobs involve driving to an office, sitting at a desk and tapping on a keyboard, before driving home again and sinking, exhausted, into the sofa. In this context, the importance of our bodies and movement is easily forgotten.

Exercise is Optional, Movement is Fundamental

Exercise is a modern invention, something designed to make up for an increasing lack of movement in our everyday lives. Movement is as old as the hills. You evolved to move: to hunt for food, to run from predators, to climb. These are all movements that helped the human body evolve in the way it did, and the result is an awesome system. However, like all systems, it requires movement and consistent usage if it is to remain in a good state of repair. Fitness used to come from movement, for many today it comes from exercise.

Gradually, an increasing number of people are beginning to realise that we need more than exercise. The rise of "functional training" is encouraging, but even more than that, we need movement. In particular, we need *conscious* movement.

Functional training often lacks a willingness to "pick the client up at the station at which they start", and overcomplicates the instructions in an attempt to appear sophisticated. It does not help when trainers lack the training or the willingness to work with their clients' Physical, Mental and Emotional State Pillars. Similarly, I have encountered many clients who, armed with their internet knowledge, request certain movements, totally ignoring the fact that their current body posture is a major impediment to performing the movements successfully and safely. The current fashionable desire to do deadlifts and squats is a case in point. Rushing out to do these movements when you have tight hips, hamstrings and a weak lower back is a recipe for disaster.

THE SEVEN BASIC MOVEMENT PATTERNS

Our bodies are designed to be able to move forward, backward and sideways, to jump up and lower down as well as to twist, all in pursuit of making our lives functional. In a functional body, there are seven basic, frequently performed movement patterns: the squat, push, bend, pull, lunge, twist, and gait (a person's manner of walking).[7] If you are serious about having your whole system function effectively, then this is the place to start. As we shall see in Part III, we can go on to take these movements further and to customise them to develop certain leadership capacities, but for now, let's start with the fundamentals.

---

7   These movement patterns were crystallised by exercise expert and physiologist Paul Chek as
     Primal Pattern® movements in his 2004 book *How to Eat, Move and Be Healthy!: Your Personalized
     4-Step Guide to Looking and Feeling Great from the Inside Out.*

1. **Squat**

    The squat is a movement where you lower your body by pushing your hips back and bending your legs. Simple everyday versions of this movement pattern include sitting down in a chair and standing up again, and squatting down to speak to a little child.

2. **Push**

    The push is a movement pattern where you move external weight away from your body. Daily activities involving this movement include pushing yourself off the ground to get up and pushing a trolley at the supermarket.

3. **Bend**

    The bend is a movement pattern where you bend your torso; the hinging motion is in your hips. This is a very common movement that we use every day, for example when we bend over to pick up a box from the floor or to lace up your shoes.

4. **Pull**

    The pull is a movement pattern where you move a weight towards your body. An everyday version of this movement is opening a door by pulling it towards your body.

5. **Twist**

    The twisting movement involves exercises where you rotate your torso, for example when you twist your body in order to throw a ball or when you twist to reach a cabinet behind your chair.

6. **Lunge**

    The lunge motion is a movement pattern that involves lowering your body by stepping one leg forward while the other leg remains stationary. A common example of this movement is walking on the stairs; a not-so-common example would be getting down on one knee to propose!

7. **Gait**

   This is the most frequently used movement pattern in our everyday lives. When you walk, jog or sprint, you are involving your gait, which combines the other movement patterns to propel your body forward.

We all *exercise* for different reasons, but whatever your goals, if you create a plan around these seven basic types of *movement*, then you will be establishing a solid platform from which to launch your own personal leadership. These seven movements are the foundation from which everything else springs.

POSTURE AWARENESS

NASM defines the purpose of posture as:

> *"to maintain enough structural efficiency to overcome
> constant forces placed on the body."*[8]

The analogy with effectiveness in other fields is obvious: if we can create an environment where all elements are aligned and moving in an efficient manner towards the goal, then there is a far greater chance of achieving success. Similarly, a team might be said to have good "posture" if it moves towards its goals in an aligned and efficient manner.

When I work with my clients, it is by paying attention to their posture and form that I can begin to identify their current habits and practices. Once you reach a certain age, your body will have developed many habits that have now become transparent to you, and as we have seen, because your Physical, Mental and Emotional State Pillars are all so closely interrelated, this is a critical factor to highlight to a client if they want to be able to make meaningful and sustainable changes in their life. However, the majority of the clients I encounter do not want to bother with this! Instead they come in full of bravado with a "go hard or go home" attitude and want to "power through" a workout, paying precious little

8   NASM. *NASM Essentials of Personal Fitness Training.*

attention to form and posture. This is a great way to keep physiotherapists and surgeons busy!

One of the things that I look to do when I am working with clients is to have them become aware of their current posture and form as well as the mental or emotional factors that shape the posture, before we work to change it. I have learned over time that raising someone's awareness in this way significantly impacts their ability to make the desired new movements with ease. Once I intervene to raise the client's awareness of their current thinking, impacting their Mental State Pillar, then they seem to find it much easier to begin to make new changes to their Physical State Pillar. It is almost as though the body will self-correct when the awareness is there. As with much of the rest of this book, the key is to slow down, become aware of current patterns and experiences, listen to the needs of your physical state, and then go from there. You might have heard this saying: "You are free to choose but you are not free from the consequence of your choice." This is just as true with regard to your body and the choices you make in the Physical State Pillar.

Consider the gestures that you habitually make: that nod, that little look down when people approach you, the way you stand, the way you lean to one side, cross your legs, etc. Over time, these gestures develop into your posture. Now consider your posture. Do you make yourself shorter or taller? Are you shrinking or upright? Can you begin to identify your repeated gestures that have created this posture? What does this posture tell you? How does it impact your Emotional and Mental State Pillars? Is this posture still serving you? Do you experience any physical, mental or emotional pain associated with your posture? If so, then how is it impacting your effectiveness, personally and/or as a leader? What will you do about it?

14

MOVEMENT AND STRESS

One of the biggest factors that inhibits freedom and range of movement is retained stress. The stress may be generated in any or all of your Physical, Mental or Emotional State Pillars, but wherever it starts, it will be held somewhere in your body. Your body has a memory every bit as much as your brain. You have probably heard of the term "muscle memory" being used in sports, and your body retains stress in the same way. You will feel it as tension or contraction and the longer you hold it, the more your freedom and range of movement become constrained. Gradually, as you learn to work around this constraint, it becomes "normal" to you and quickly disappears from your awareness, leaving you with an invisible restriction. There are many techniques you can practise to relieve stress, but there is one technique in particular we have found that really works to eliminate the retained stress at source.

TRE® (TRAUMA & TENSION RELEASE EXERCISE)

Some years ago, we were introduced to this wonderful form of movement called TRE® (Trauma & Tension Release Exercise) by our good friend and co-trainer at NFA, Chris Balsley. Developed by Dr. David Berceli, this is a series of movements that occur in your Physical State Pillar and yet also have powerful consequences in your Emotional and Mental State Pillars.

The exercises are very simple. You carry out a short series of five movements designed to fatigue the muscles that habitually contract under stress. Most of these reside in the lower body and the lower back. In particular, the exercises target the psoas muscle, the muscle that connects the lower and upper body and is responsible for the automatic contraction your body performs when it is startled or frightened. Once this series of movements has been completed, you simply lie down on the floor, push the soles of your feet together and allow your body to do what it wants to do when your muscles are fatigued: shake! The process is fascinating as you can experience the interplay of the three Internal Pillars at work in real time:

- Physical State Pillar: "My body wants to shake."
- Mental State Pillar: "Shaking means I am vulnerable. It means I cannot cope."
- Emotional State Pillar: "I am scared/embarrassed to shake."

At some point, if you have successfully fatigued your muscles in the first part of the process, you will experience some minor trembles, and over time these trembles will develop and spread throughout your body. As this happens, the concerns of your Mental and Emotional State Pillars diminish and the requirements of your Physical State Pillar come to the fore.

Everyone shakes differently. There is no one right way. The principle is this: mammals automatically contract and instigate their sympathetic nervous system when they are stressed or frightened. Consider how you react when you hear a sudden loud noise. Your immediate and automatic response is to flinch and contract your body. What Dr. Berceli noticed was that when the danger had passed, non-human mammals and children physically "shook off" the experience, whilst adult humans did not. They seemed unwilling to shake and instead, therefore retained the shock in their body. What he postulated was that the requirements of the Physical State Pillar to shake it off were overridden by the needs of the Emotional and Mental State Pillars to "keep your stuff together", "never let them see you sweat", etc.

Shaking in human history has long had a bad press: in times past it might get you drowned as a witch or strung up as being possessed by the devil. In the 21st century, if you shake, people assess you as being "unable to cope" or "emotionally unstable", both of which are major "crimes" in today's world. The result of this has been to resist the naturally designed physical process of "shaking off the stress", and therefore people are walking around today pent up with unresolved stress in their body. The more you try and resist the desire to shake, the bigger the stress gets. Isn't it always the case? What you resist persists! You never deal with it, you avoid it, and while you avoid it, maybe it dissipates a little, but then *boom*, it comes back again, magnified ten-fold! Sound familiar?

Many other mechanisms have been devised to try and defuse stress: exercise, food, drugs, meditation, etc., and they all work to a greater or lesser degree for a certain amount of time. However, TRE® aims to deal with the stress at source, by completing the natural, physical state process, as the body was designed: to feel the stress, contract, survive the stressful period *and then shake it off.*

TRE® is one more example which shows that all three of your Internal Pillars are highly integrated and that we ignore the Physical State Pillar at our peril. Our bodies are designed to move, and when we overlook or resist the needs of the Physical State Pillar, we are operating at a diminished capacity.

PERSONAL REFLECTION

Marcus: TRE®

My own personal experience with TRE® was very revealing. I have a long-standing disc problem right at the bottom of my spine, the result of playing too much cricket as a schoolboy. As a result of this, I have always (consciously or not) protected that side of my back, and been very careful with certain movements. My Mental State Pillar told me that this protectiveness was the "right" thing to do. When I lay down on the floor to do my TRE® after a few initial sessions, I finally learned to "turn off" the controlling rational part of my brain and let my body take over. What it did next was very revealing and left a big impression on me: it basically shook all over the place and had me do movements that my Mental State Pillar would never have let me do! In that moment, I experientially discovered the innate wisdom of my Physical State Pillar: my body knew where it needed to shake and expel the tension that I had been holding onto for many years.

Learning to pay attention to my body and assign more importance to my Physical State Pillar has been a large part of my journey ever since. I woke up to the fact that for many years, I had prioritised my Mental and Emotional State Pillars at the expense of my Physical State Pillar and what my body was trying to tell me. This remains a journey for me. The old patterns are strong, but over time, I am learning to pay attention to the physical cues that arise from my body.

PERSONAL REFLECTION

Sari: TRE®

My own experience with TRE® began with skepticism. I was a physical trainer. I knew about the body. I could exercise my stress away. What was the problem with what I was doing all along? Did I really need TRE®?

As a result, I really did not shake much at all in my first few attempts. It was only when I really allowed myself to relax and trust the process that I began to experience the tremors. My shaking was more a vibration, in contrast to Marcus's rather more violent movements (I guess it is rather stressful to be married to me!), and I worried about that for a while, but again, once I relaxed and learnt to trust the wisdom of my body, things really began to happen for me.

Although my shakes have never become large, I have experienced a real lengthening of my torso, as a result of TRE®. The more my mental state relaxed, the more my body took over and the more "free" I felt. The TRE® experience has been very liberating for me and now I have moved from being a skeptic to being a certified TRE® trainer. It is a method that I love to use, especially with women, as so many of them, like me, seem to experience a sense of liberation and freedom as a result of regular TRE® practice.

In my daily life as a coach, especially in my interactions with others, TRE® has helped me learn to relax. TRE® practice also compliments my strength by widening my range of motion and emotion. I have become both a better listener and a better mover as a result.

EUSTRESS AND DISTRESS

Practising TRE® is a wonderful way to reduce the impact of stress that is retained in your Physical, Mental and Emotional State Pillars. However, stress per se is not a bad thing; far from it, in fact. For example, when you exercise, you are physically stressing your system. Stress is one of *the* most misunderstood and wrongfully-vilified areas of modern life. How many articles have you read with headlines such as "Stress: The Number One Killer of the 21st Century", for example? It is important to understand that stress, in and of itself, is not a killer at all. In fact, stress is a fundamental and critical part of living, growing and developing. However, ongoing, unrelenting stress, retained in your system, *is* a killer.

There is an important distinction between what the scientists call "eustress" and "distress". The *eu-* prefix meaning "good" in Greek, "eustress" refers to good stress, and we all know that "distress" is bad stress. It is the *person's reaction* to the stressor that determines whether something is classified as eustress or distress. A simple way to understand the distinction is that if someone reacts to a situation as a *challenge*, then it results in eustress, whereas if they begin to perceive the situation as *threatening* or even *overwhelming*, then the stress becomes distress.

It is critical to understand that eustress is necessary for peak performance.

Figure 14.1 Stress to Performance Scale

The Stress to Performance Scale (Figure 14.1) clearly illustrates the point: Too little stress results in boredom and low levels of performance. Performance peaks when a manageable level of stress is experienced, but quickly disintegrates when that stress becomes overwhelming and *un*manageable. If you ever have felt that indefinable feeling of being "in the zone" or "flow", then you have experienced eustress. In this situation, you might even feel that you can take on the world! However, when you experience being out of control, with no end in sight and you perceive the situation is being forced on you, then that is when distress kicks in, all hope is extinguished and you cannot see a way out. The enhanced performance of the eustress stage quickly evaporates and is replaced by a feeling of hopelessness and helplessness.

Exercise can be a wonderful way to experience eustress, although of course, if you force yourself to exercise and hate every minute of it, then you can quickly turn eustress into distress. There is nothing magical in exercise, but correctly used, it can be a great way to build the capacity to experience "good stress" and, just as importantly, the capacity to recover from it.

Exercise and Stress

When you exercise, your body experiences stress and responds by releasing the stress hormone called cortisol. This hormone is released by the adrenal gland and increases glucose concentration in the blood, thereby giving you more energy to overcome the stressor, whatever it might be. Over-exercising and overstimulating in general can lead to the overproduction of cortisol, which in turn leads to fat production, weight gain, brain decline and a breakdown in the function of the immune system. It is also catabolic, which means it breaks down muscle and looks to preserve carbohydrate and deliver energy to your system.

In small, occasional doses, however, cortisol is extremely useful as it enables you to overcome stressful situations, injury and illness. In fact, your body is not only designed to cope with stress, it actually *requires* stress if it is to perform to its ultimate capacity!

The willingness to exercise and the consequent cycle of stress and recovery/restoration is a huge factor in peak perfomance. However, *both* factors are *equally* important: stress *and* recovery/restoration. One without the other, or an imbalance between them, can lead to problems.

It is important to realise that the desire to eliminate stress
from your life is not a healthy goal!

Although we have been talking in the domain of the Physical State Pillar here, it is just as important in the Mental and Emotional State Pillars. A life without stress is a life of suboptimal performance. A life full of unrelenting stress is a life of weight gain (or weight loss), sickness and despair!

Heart Health and Stress

If you have ever had a cardiac health check, you may now be starting to join up the dots. The way that a doctor tests your cardiac health is to put you on a treadmill and stress your heart to a certain level while monitoring how long it takes to reach that level. Once the level is reached, the doctor then gets you off the treadmill and measures how long your heart takes to go back to its original resting rate. They measure this in terms of beats per minute. The *slower* your heart takes to reach the appropriate stress level, the healthier it is. The *quicker* your heart can return to its original starting point, the healthier it is.

Now apply that thinking to the stress you experience in your life. We have already seen why the complete avoidance of all stress is not a good target, and similarly, that prolonged exposure to stress is equally damaging. So, given that some level of stress is desirable, consider how you would *like* to deal with stress.

Option 1: Quick to get distressed and slow to recover.
Option 2: Quick to get distressed and quick to recover.
Option 3: Slow to get distressed and slow to recover.
Option 4: Slow to get distressed and quick to recover.

Option 4 offers the best of both worlds. While you take some time to *become* distressed (you don't fly off the handle at every little inconvenience), you are quick to recover from it and regain your equilibrium. You and your system experience the benefits of stress, but you don't get stuck in it. This is exactly the same logic as the cardiac health test: slow to reach the point of distress, but quick to return to the "normal" state.

15

HIGH INTENSITY INTERVAL TRAINING

According to sport and exercise psychologist Dr. J. Kip Matthews, "exercise affords the body an opportunity to practise responding to stress, streamlining the communication between the systems involved in the stress response. The less active we become, the more challenged we are in dealing with stress."[9]

There is one form of exercise that is particularly useful in this context: high intensity interval training (HIIT). It goes by many other names: Tabata training, sprint interval training, etc., but all these different forms share something in common: a rapid and repeated pattern of stress and recovery. This pattern

---

9   Domonell, Kristen. "Why Endorphins (and Exercise) Make You Happy." *CNN*, edition.cnn.com/2016/01/13/health/endorphins-exercise-cause-happiness.

is extremely useful not only physiologically, but also because it embodies and develops in the practitioner the capacity to experience stress and discomfort and then recover from it. As we have seen, this capacity is highly important in personal development and leadership development in particular. If you are not willing to experience stress and discomfort then you will never maximise your development, personally or as a leader. However, if you do not also develop the capacity to *recover* quickly from that stress and discomfort, then you will not reap the benefits of the stress you have experienced.

There are many types of interval training and you can vary the intervals of stress and recovery ad infinitum, however, to reap the maximum benefits then you do need to be willing to experience a *significant* level of stress and discomfort before you begin the recovery cycle. In addition, the recovery cycle cannot be so long as to allow for complete recovery.

Nowadays, driven by the increasing number of "wearables" offered by companies such as Apple, Polar, Garmin, etc., it is becoming ever easier to track your heart rate. Some of these are a lot more accurate than others. If you intend to use a heart rate monitor for HIIT, then use a reputable brand with a chest strap. These are far more accurate than monitors that take readings via the wrist. There is a whole science behind this: there are specific heart rate zones to be calculated, etc. This is not the place to go into the calculations in great detail (a quick internet search can help you with that), but suffice to say that establishing your resting heart rate, calculating your maximum heart rate and the zones in between is a very good start!

IMPORTANT

Before you dive headlong into any form of exercise, especially a high impact methodology such as HIIT, it is very important that you consult a doctor and get medical clearance.

STRESS, YOUR BRAIN AND INTELLIGENCE

What is especially exciting and becoming increasingly well-established is that if you are willing to experience these short intense periods of stress, your brain goes into overdrive and it starts producing a protein called the brain-derived neurotrophic factor (BDNF).[10] Scientists are still learning about this protein, but it is already clear that BDNF is a very powerful factor in facilitating long-term memory, learning and higher-level thinking. The bottom line:

If you are willing to experience significant discomfort and then allow yourself time and space to recover from it, then you end up making yourself smarter!

So, let's be really clear: when you say, "I don't have time to exercise", what you are really saying is, "I don't have time to get smarter". Ouch!

SPRINTING

To sprint: "to move at full speed over a short distance". When was the last time you sprinted? Marcus loves this question. Young children sprint all the time. You were a young child once. What happened? If you said, "I got old", then that is a cop out! While that is true, it does not answer the question. Whatever your age, you still have a "full speed"—when did you stop using it? Why?

Sprinting hurts. It is one of the most uncomfortable things you can do. It is lung-bustingly, muscle-stretchingly uncomfortable. Not only that, but you don't look particularly cool while you are doing it and you generally look even less cool while you are recovering from it immediately afterwards (unless you are Usain Bolt). It is uncomfortable in every domain! Your Physical, Mental and Emotional State Pillars are all shaken up when you sprint.

Young kids sprint because something matters enough to get there fast. They are focussed on their purpose—to reach their target as quickly as possible—rather than the experience of getting there, or how they look while they get there.

---

10   I first became aware of the BDNF protein and the way in which strenuous exercise can stimulate it while reading *Spark: The Revolutionary New Science of Exercise and the Brain* by John J. Ratey.

PERSONAL REFLECTION

Marcus: Sprinting

When I am walking to the gym, knowing that I am about to do some sprinting sessions, the mental and emotional stress kicks in even before the physical stress begins!

Most of the time, I do my interval sprint training on a treadmill, but occasionally I will do it outside, and it is amusing to watch people's reaction. While they are used to seeing people jog around at a comfortable pace, they are generally less familiar with seeing someone tear past at full speed and then stop to recover, and then sprint again! People seem to assume that something is wrong (with me?) when they see me sprint. Somehow, sprinting is linked with the presence of emergency or danger, because, surely, only an emergency or danger would justify breaking out of your comfortable cocoon, right?

The Good News and the Bad News

Sprinting (followed by recovery) offers wonderful benefits to your Physical, Mental and Emotional State Pillars. However, it *does not* look cool and it *does* hurt. So, if you notice that you have not sprinted recently (and if you notice that even now, after reading this, you still have no intention of incorporating some sprinting into your life), at least be honest with yourself: being comfortable and looking cool are more important to you than learning, growth, development and peak performance. It does not mean you are a bad person in any way, but at least be honest with yourself.

To be clear, sprinting in this context does not need to involve *running*. Sprinting means to *move* at full speed. So, you can "sprint" on a stationary bike, on a cross trainer, a rowing machine, in a swimming pool, etc; the possibilities are endless. A good way to choose your form of HIIT exercise is to factor in your body type. As we shall see in Chapter 21, your basic body type plays a big part in many areas of your life, but for now just consider that if you are leaner and narrow in build then running can be a good choice, if you are wider and rounder in build then a lower impact exercise like the cross-trainer is easier on the joints, whereas if you tend to have a more middling build then a full-body workout such as the rowing machine is a good choice.

So, when *was* the last time you sprinted? The answer will be very revealing regarding your willingness to experience discomfort.

LIFE: A SERIES OF SPRINTS OR A MARATHON?

Interval training also provides a wonderful way to embody a powerful attitude towards life if you are concerned with peak performance. When I am coaching people, one of the biggest factors I see that holds them back is their attitude or how they are approaching life as a whole. This is one of things that it is very hard to spot for yourself until you work with a coach, because it functions quietly in the background, seemingly not doing very much, when in fact it controls *everything*: how you think, how you feel and what you do. Your Physical, Mental and Emotional State Pillars are all essentially a product of your attitude towards life and your attitude towards life is essentially a product of your Physical, Mental and Emotional State Pillars!

Here is the distinction to which I am pointing: some people live their life as though it is one long marathon, while some see it as a series of sprints and recovery sessions. This has profound implications for how they live their life and what they experience in their Mental, Physical and Emotional Pillars. They think, move and feel differently, according to how they see life.

Life as a Marathon

The people whom I coach that approach life as a marathon tend to have certain characteristics: they move slower, are constantly tired, stressed and tend to have more health issues. They speak of the experience of a never-ending battle to keep their head above water or to keep ahead of the chasing pack. They also tend to feel guilty about taking a break, which usually results in being overwhelmed. As a result, they tend to try and avoid stress, because they don't see any possibility for recovery. They seek to avoid distress and as a result, eliminate the critical experience of eustress in the process.

Life as a Series of Sprints

People who see life as a series of sprints and recovery periods see life very differently, and as a result, have a very different experience of life. They tend to have more energy, be more excited about challenges and are more "upbeat" in general. They are less concerned with beating/competing against other people and are more focussed on being the best that *they* can be. Crucially, they push themselves to go further and faster. *They are not concerned with conserving energy as they play the game, because they know there is a recovery period around the corner.*

These people actively seek out periods of eustress, and as we saw earlier in this section, eustress is a critical enabler of peak performance. These people avoid distress by recovering just as hard as they seek eustress.

"Life is beautiful, as long as it consumes you.
When it is rushing through you, destroying you, life is gorgeous, glorious.
It's when you burn a slow fire and save fuel, that life's not worth having."
- D. H. Lawrence, *A Modern Lover*

Envision this: you are standing on a stationary treadmill. How do you decide how fast to run? It depends on how long you intend to run before you take a break. If you set the timer for an hour, then you are going to run at a relatively slow pace and most likely experience some boredom along the way. Even if you do not experience boredom, notice where your satisfaction occurs: at the end of the hour—you survived! Congratulations! Contrast that with setting the timer for 20 minutes, divided into one-minute intervals. Now, you can afford to blast out of the blocks, go 100%, experience eustress, recover and go 100% again. Notice where the satisfaction occurs in this example. Now, it occurs at the end of each individual sprint *and* at the end of the session.

Now, imagine that treadmill is your life or your career. If you see the timer set to one long period of 30 years, then you are going to approach it rather differently than if you see it set to a series of shorter intervals that, when taken together, add up to 30 years. This is also true at a more micro level: do you see a day as one long run or are you willing to split it up into a series of shorter "sprints" that you intersperse with short restoration breaks?

The Hare and the Tortoise

Do you remember Aesop's old fable "The Hare and the Tortoise"? The hare and the tortoise agree to a race. The hare is cocky and sprints off at a fast pace, while the quietly confident tortoise plods along at a slow, steady pace. But the cocky hare decides to take a nap halfway and gets overtaken by the tortoise, who wins the race!

For hundreds of years, this has been taken to show that "slow and steady wins the race", but this is not the case at all. The reason that the tortoise beat the hare is that the hare tried to sprint the whole way, experienced distress and exhaustion and had to take a nap to recover before it could continue the race! If the hare had taken regular recovery breaks to smell the roses after each sprint, then it would have comfortably beaten the tortoise! Sorry, Aesop!

EMBODYING INTERVAL TRAINING

Regular interval training is a fantastic way to learn and really get to "know" this approach to life in an embodied way, rather than as a concept or an idea. Again, the importance of the body in adopting this attitude towards life cannot be overstated. You can read about it in a book like this, engaging your Mental State Pillar forever and a day, but until you *practise* it, engaging your Physical State Pillar, then nothing much is really going to happen for you.

Interval training is not the only beneficial form of exercise, of course. In Part III, we will greatly expand this notion of how different kinds of movement and exercise can build different capacities and experiences that will support you in your leadership. It is fascinating and liberating to experience the impact that the Physical State Pillar can have on your Emotional and Mental State Pillars.

16

EXERCISE

In my role as a physical trainer, although I often begin by working with the Physical and Mental State Pillars, I am often struck that my most lasting impact is in the domain of the Emotional State Pillar. For instance, once somebody is standing taller and with her shoulders comfortably rolled back, then suddenly they report feeling emotions such as confidence, joy and power, and this impact is felt throughout their whole life.

Your whole life story (Physical, Mental and Emotional State Pillars) is contained in your body, its form and its posture. Certain emotions and beliefs simply do not exist in certain postures and forms. You can experience that for yourself very easily: if you contract your body now, slump over and let your eyes focus on the floor, sighing all the while, then it is very difficult to feel joyful. In contrast, if you stand tall, establish eye contact, throw your shoulders back and smile, then it is very difficult to feel sad. Your Physical, Mental and Emotional State Pillars combine to form an overall coherency: they are consistent and fit together like the pieces in a jigsaw puzzle.

Whatever you have practised thinking (Mental State Pillar) and feeling (Emotional State Pillar) up until this point in your life will be reflected in your body (Physical State Pillar). One analogy that I like to use in this area is that your body is the publisher of your life story! Everyone likes to focus on "body language" and the *external messages* that you may or may not be sending, but I am more concerned with the *internal processes* that are the result of your Mental and Emotional State Pillars and that are being reflected in your posture.

There are a million books and webpages out there on the importance of exercising and almost everyone knows that they "should" exercise. Some are even aware that the benefits of exercise are more than simply physical. There are huge benefits that can be experienced in the domain of the Emotional and Mental State Pillars. There is little point in regurgitating that mantra here. Once again, understanding that something is a good idea does not necessarily lead to committed action.

EXERCISE AND LEADERSHIP

With exercise and leadership, the slant is a little different because we are not looking at how and why exercise is important in general terms, but rather why it is a critical factor in personal development, and in particular, leadership. It is a well-established fact that exercising impacts your health, but it is less well-attested that it can help your development as a leader. As discussed in the first section of this book, while physical athletes have been quick to pick up on the importance of mental and emotional states if they want to win, the reverse has been much more slowly, even grudgingly, accepted; namely, that if you want to win in the "mental" or "non-physical" world of business, for example, then not only does your emotional state make a difference, but your physical state does too.

At a very basic level, this is obvious: if you are physically sick, unable to move or get out of bed, then it becomes a lot harder to lead. I know many of you are thinking of exceptions like Stephen Hawking and you are right—it is not impossible to be physically challenged *and* be a leader. However, what I am concerned with here is to take a look at how physical exercise can aid your development and learning, and give you an edge when it comes to leadership.

EXERCISE AND PHYSIOLOGY

At a basic, physiological level, exercise has many benefits which go beyond improving the physical state. Exercise:

- pumps blood to your brain, helping to boost its overall performance.
- develops chemicals that support a healthy hippocampus (the part of your brain that supports memory and learning).
- releases endorphins and serotonin: the feel-good chemicals you have probably heard about.
- increases concentrations of norepinephrine, a chemical that improves the brain's response to stress.

There is a myriad of other biological factors that are also improved by exercise, but as the focus of this book is not biology, I will not go into details. The above benefits should present a compelling enough case for you to start exercising!

EXERCISE AND LEADERSHIP CAPACITIES

So, aside from pure biology, how does exercise play a part in leadership development? Surely they are very different things? At one level, they *are* very different: one is a largely physical activity, while the other does not seem to require much physical effort or use of the body at all. However, as we shall see in Part III, exercise can play a major role in helping to develop critical leadership capacities.

But before we go there, we will start with a really basic example and one that is at the heart of what impedes many people's willingness and ability to exercise and lead: namely, the capacity to "get uncomfortable".

COMFORT AND DISCOMFORT

As we saw in Part I where Marcus outlined the idea of the comfort zone, the desire for the feeling of comfort is a major driver of human behaviour today. Think of all the technological innovations that have happened in the past 50 years: the vast majority of them are specifically designed to make your life more comfortable. That is at once a blessing and a curse.

Air conditioning, dishwashers, mobile phones, the internet, are just some examples of the fantastic innovations that increase your level of comfort (well, except when they break down!). However, these developments have created a sense of entitlement towards comfort, and the resulting aversion to being uncomfortable is also a curse for those interested in developing their leadership capacity. Why? Because leadership, by definition, not only requires you to go to new places and experience new things, but also for you to take other people there too. Leadership will require you to step outside your comfort zone and take risks. Inherent in that process is the willingness to get uncomfortable, perhaps in the domain of the Mental State Pillar (being open to beliefs different from your own), in the domain of the Emotional State Pillar (being willing to feel emotions that you had previously resisted experiencing) or in the domain of the Physical State Pillar (being willing to present your body in a new way), or maybe in all three domains at once!

Exercise involves getting uncomfortable. It is just part of the deal. As Jim Rohn once famously said:

"You can't hire someone else to do your push-ups for you."

I have heard pretty much every excuse under the sun for not exercising, and I would say that about 90% of them boil down to this: "I don't want to get uncomfortable".

If nothing else, the willingness to commit to regular exercise is a wonderful way to build the capacity for getting uncomfortable, dealing with it, and dare I even say, *enjoy* it! As we saw earlier, if you want to "learn" discomfort and "know" it, then it has to live for you, in your *body*—not as a mental concept, but as something you have physically practised.

> *If you want to grow, learn and ultimately develop as a leader in life,*
> *then you will need to develop the capacity to get uncomfortable.*

Exercise is one fantastic way to develop that capacity for yourself, not as a nice idea in your brain, but as a real entity in your whole system: mentally, emotionally and physically.

Discomfort and the Body

Your body or physical state is often the easiest place to intervene if you want to build the capacity to experience discomfort. If you intervene with your mental state or thought process, then experiencing discomfort involves being willing to be wrong about your beliefs. That is not very popular with human beings— we prefer to be *right*. The other option is to practise experiencing emotional discomfort. Once again, that is not an experience for which many human beings actually clamour!

So, that just leaves us with the body, where experiencing discomfort really means just getting out of breath and maybe a few sore limbs the morning after. It is still uncomfortable, but for most people, it is often the least of the three "evils". As we have already seen with HIIT, different forms of exercise create different levels of discomfort, and the body is very quick to adapt, so *how* you exercise is also important in this area. It is perfectly possible to exercise and experience minimal discomfort.

Comfort & Speed Matrix

Before we look any further, let's examine this whole area of comfort and discomfort a little more in the Comfort & Speed Matrix exercise (Figure 16.1):

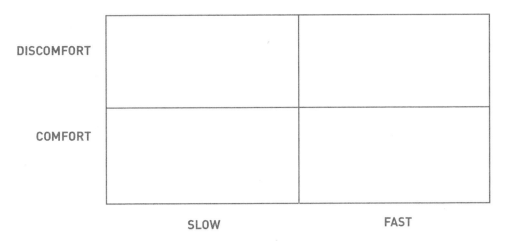

DISCOMFORT

COMFORT

SLOW   FAST

Figure 16.1 Comfort & Speed Matrix

Consider different elements of your life and place them on the above matrix. It can be a very revealing exercise. The speed at which you do things is often directly linked to the level of discomfort you are willing to endure. For example, running slowly will keep me comfortable, whereas running fast will make me uncomfortable. However, eating fast can quickly remove the discomfort of hunger, while eating slowly can be a nuisance because it causes me discomfort elsewhere in my life. We will return to the importance of the speed of your eating in Chapter 19! As another example, take the speed at which I learn: I feel more comfortable when I am learning quickly than when I am learning slowly, even though "slow" learning may, in the end, be more effectively retained. Lifting weights quickly is a lot more comfortable than lifting them slowly.

The fast and comfortable zone is the zone of the 21st century. I want to do everything quickly and with minimal discomfort. I want all the benefit as fast as possible and I want it without feeling any discomfort.

What is revealing for you to notice in your life is where your next favourite box is. Do you prioritise speed over comfort or vice versa? If you can't have "it" (whatever "it" is) fast and with minimal discomfort, then do you prefer to slow down and maintain your comfort level, or do you prefer to stay fast and endure some discomfort?

While there is value in all four of those boxes, the slow and comfortable zone is often a trap that my clients fall into, as it, on its own, can lead to stagnation. The slow speed and the comfortable experience can seem very inviting, but it can also quickly lead to boredom.

On the other hand, the slow and uncomfortable zone, while extremely unfashionable in the 21st century, can be the source of powerful and sustained learning. This is where the idea of "apprenticeship" lives. It may not be very sexy, but the willingness to move slowly and in the process experience discomfort is often at the heart of sustained learning and knowledge. Similarly, lifting a weight slowly is a good way to experience maximum discomfort but it also produces major growth in the long term.

The fast and uncomfortable zone is also a powerful area to explore in your life. Where are you willing to compromise your love of comfort by being willing to step up the pace?

Consider how these two dimensions apply to you. What do you notice? What does that show about how you are living your life? Where has the desire to be comfortable or fast overshadowed your desire to grow and develop? As we will see later on, it is very often the willingness to consciously shift between these various boxes that can provide the biggest, most sustained developments of all.

The Importance of Comfort

Now, I am not saying that "discomfort" is *better than* "comfort". As we shall see, they both have their role to play in learning, growth and development; however, in the 21st century, the drive to feel comfortable has become such a pervasive force that it is important to begin to redress the balance and point out the importance of "discomfort" in the whole process.

For some people, discomfort can even become comfortable! These are the "adrenaline junkies", and this book is certainly not advocating that as a way forward. It is the willingness to consciously choose to experience both discomfort *and* comfort that is the key.

17

BREAKING HABITS

Closely linked to the importance of discomfort is the importance of breaking habits. One of the reasons human beings form habits is to reduce the irritation and discomfort of doing new things. As such, we create patterns everywhere in our lives. Habits show up in all three Internal Pillars: they exist in the Physical, Mental and Emotional State Pillars; patterns exist in the domains of movement, thinking and feeling. As we get older, our beliefs harden into facts, our emotions become moods and our once-flexible joints become stiff. All of these can be mitigated by the willingness to notice and break habits.

While these patterns provide convenience and comfort, they also keep us trapped, for just as surely as our input remains the same, so will our output, in the form of our results. This is one reason why children learn, develop and grow so much faster than adults: they have no patterns and habits to hold them back. Certainly there is nothing wrong with habits and patterns, but unless you are willing to break them, your future will look very much like your past. In fact, one of the most important habits to cultivate is that of breaking habits! The capacity to break habits is a capacity that can be developed just like any other, and just like any other habit, you create it by doing it, not by thinking about it.

Habits can also be something that I *never* do. Today, the habit of not exercising is one such very popular habit. Why? Because as we have seen, exercise involves discomfort, and many people in the 21st century like to avoid discomfort like our forebears liked to avoid the plague!

WALKING AND BREATHING

Some of the simplest and yet most impactful habits on which to intervene lie in the domain of the Physical State Pillar. One powerful example: walking and breathing. Our good friend and colleague at NFA, Beatriz Garcia, introduced us to a very simple way to practice intervening in both of these areas simultaneously via an easy practice.

To do this, all you need do is walk around the room, breathing in when you move your left leg until your left foot hits the ground, then breathing out when you move your right leg until your right foot hits the floor. As you do this exercise, you can vary the speed at which you move, which changes the speed at which you breathe. Doing this, you will notice the impact that varying the speeds of breathing and walking have on you, in all three domains. The Physical, Emotional and Mental State Pillars are all simultaneously impacted.

The more often you do something, the more transparent it becomes to you. The more transparent it becomes to you, the more "normal" it appears to you, and ultimately, the more power it has over you. You cannot change a habit that you do not know you have. This is why shifting patterns in such "routine" areas as walking and breathing can make such a powerful difference.

The world today runs at such a pace that many people's breathing has become incredibly short and shallow, characterised by a focus on inhalation, a movement that fires up the sympathetic nervous system, which in turn activates the well-known fight or flight syndrome. That is why so many people experience being "'always on", and fuelled by caffeine and other stimulants, are experiencing the phenomenon of adrenal fatigue. By way of contrast, the experience of breathing out activates the parasympathetic nervous system and its rather less famous "rest and digest" function (because who has got time for *that*?!). But it is actually this "rest and digest" function that helps your body maintain its balance and recover from stress.

Your breathing pattern is a great example of a habit that gets developed at a very early age and then forgotten about. Intervening on those types of habits can have profound impacts on your physical, mental and emotional states. One such recent example of this showed up with one of Marcus's clients.

CLIENT CASE STUDY

Fotis Kampouris, VP of Operations, Emerging Countries, Inspection at Lloyd's Register, working with Marcus

When I first met Fotis, he was in an interesting position. He was still producing great results, but he was in danger of burning himself out. He was running flat out and the cracks were beginning to show. It takes a brave man to reconfigure himself when his results do not demand it, but this is exactly what Fotis did.

Fotis later told me that during our first meeting, his initial expectation of executive coaching was for me to tell him how to fix his problems. However, over the course of our coaching sessions, he soon discovered the power of observing himself and connecting his physical state with his mental and emotional states. By allowing himself to be open and present during these sessions, Fotis discovered emotional and physical habits that he had developed over many years. This revelation helped him develop powerful new practices, which in turn developed his capacity for new actions and created the opportunity for him to recover and come out on top before he burned himself out.

One of the first things we worked on together was to help him develop more *range*. We began with his breathing patterns: Fotis, like many executives with whom I work, had unconsciously developed a habit of taking short, shallow and fast breaths. As a result, his whole system was "pumped" and this was showing up in his Emotional State Pillar, where he was emotionally volatile, and his Mental State Pillar, where he believed his assessments to be assertions. Intervening via his Physical State Pillar has had a big impact on his Emotional and Mental State Pillars.

Fotis realised that he was able to "centre himself" by breathing slowly and deeply during times of stress, and that this helped him look differently at his situation and discover new possibilities. Together with the other practices that Fotis has learnt, this breathing practice has enabled him to manage his stress levels, improve his time management and most importantly, get a handle on the expectations he places on himself and on others.

CONSCIOUS MOVEMENT

Unconscious movement, "busy-ness" or running around like a headless chicken does not provide the same focussed benefit as being conscious of your intent while you move. This is another great example of how you can obtain maximum benefit from your efforts when you link the three Internal Pillars of Performance.

Conscious movement involves harnessing the combined power of your Mental and Physical State Pillars. The key is to be conscious and aware of the movements that your body is making (or not making). You have been moving for a very long time and so the way you do it inevitably becomes invisible to you. Almost everybody I encounter in my coaching has learned to favour one side or the other, stoop or extend, contract or expand parts of their body. It is not wrong for them to do so. In fact, it is the way that they have learned to get through life. However, once this physical behaviour becomes ingrained, they become unknowingly caged in a prison of their own making. Once their body stiffens into certain positions, it begins to similarly shape how they think and feel too.

In my coaching, I do not just focus on exercise; I also focus on the quality of a person's movement in general. Where are they fluid or loose, and where are they stiff or tight? Very often their capacity to exercise is limited not just by their levels of fitness and strength but also simply by the quality of the movement that they are able to perform.

One of the things that I love about our coaching is that by working with people on things as simple as the way that they walk, bend, stretch twist and turn, they are able to create new awareness in their body. This new awareness can then become the source of learning that facilitates new purposeful and intended choices about how they will move forward in their life emotionally, mentally and physically.

THE IMPORTANCE OF REST AND RECOVERY

Since Chapter 16, I have been focussing on the importance of developing the capacity and willingness to get uncomfortable. This capacity drives growth and development, but it is only of equal importance to the capacity that you also rest and relax.

The process is important to understand: when you experience discomfort, you are stepping out of the comfort zone that Marcus discussed in Part I; you are taking a risk. It can be a risk to think differently (Mental State Pillar), feel differently (Emotional State Pillar) or move and act differently (Physical State

Pillar), and risking in one domain invariably involves also feeling discomfort in the other two!

However, growth does not happen while you are taking the risk; it happens *after* you have taken it and can reflect and integrate that new experience into your worldview and identity: "Hmm… that wasn't so bad, maybe I am a person who can speak in public, after all." Exercise provides a great parallel: when you lift weights, this causes your muscle fibres to tear and break down. It is after you complete your final rep that you start to recover: the muscle fibres re-knit and rebuild, bigger and stronger than before. This process is called hypertrophy, and you can see how it can be a powerful analogy for growth in the world of personal and leadership development. In both cases, the importance of rest and restoration is critical, because *that is when the growth occurs.*

In the case of personal development, this rest and restoration can involve micro- or macro- breaks, depending on where you focus. Macro-breaks might be going overseas for a few days or weeks of vacation, making sure that you actually *rest* on these holidays instead of constantly and compulsively checking your emails. Micro-breaks would be to allow yourself to stop and pause for 10 minutes at regular intervals during the day. Making the time to rest and recover, both on a macro-level and on a micro-level, is crucial in helping you become better at what you do.

Sleep

Sleep is a very important factor in this equation of rest and recovery. Scientists are learning more and more about the regenerative properties of sleep.

One of my favourite areas to explore with clients is to ask them to monitor the amount of sleep that they get within a week. For the first week, I do not go into details, letting them monitor their sleep however they want, and at the end of the week they give me the number of hours' sleep they think they have had. However, for the second week, I give them precise instructions on *how* to monitor the amount of sleep they get, and the number comes back a lot smaller. People generally overestimate the amount of sleep they are getting and they often confuse "hours asleep" with "hours in bed". That is not the same thing at all.

It is interesting how people set an alarm in the morning to wake them up, but they do not set an alarm in the evening to tell them to go to sleep. Try setting two alarms: one telling you to go to sleep (not to bed) and one telling you to wake up. It is an interesting way to interrupt a regular pattern in your life.

If you want to continue to learn, grow and develop as well as experience peak performance, then sleep is a critical factor in your rest and recovery practice. Remember the difference between seeing life as a marathon or a sprint. The sprint is powerful but only when it is linked with the capacity to recover.

There is another aspect that is crucial to your body's performance: nutrition. This is a critical factor that we all make choices about every single day, but unfortunately, it is only rarely discussed in the domain of personal and leadership development. In the next few chapters, Marcus will examine how nutrition and your eating habits can have a significant effect towards creating peak performance.

18

NUTRITION

Much like exercise, nutrition has only recently been allowed at the table of personal or leadership development. As development moved from the purely Mental State Pillar of what you know and began to (grudgingly) allow for the importance of your Emotional State Pillar, so it has more recently (and even more grudgingly) begun to allow for the importance of the Physical State Pillar. As we have already seen, your body, exercise and your Physical State Pillar all play important roles in your capacity to grow, learn, develop and perform at peak performance. It is no secret that your nutritional choices impact your physical body, and given that your thoughts and feelings *exist* in your physical body, it shouldn't come as a surprise that they too are impacted by what you eat and drink.

THE INFLUENCE OF NUTRITION

If you stop to consider the biggest factors that influence your Physical State Pillar, it will not be long before you come across nutrition. Throughout this book, we have stressed the dynamic interaction between the three Internal Pillars, your Physical, Emotional and Mental State Pillars. The same is true here:

- What my body requires me to eat – Physical State Pillar
- What I know I should eat – Mental State Pillar
- What I feel like eating – Emotional State Pillar

For many people the battle between these three elements is an everyday struggle, and the struggle is real!

As we have already seen elsewhere, the Emotional State Pillar is often the biggest driver behind our behaviour. It trumps the Mental State Pillar on a regular basis: I know I should eat the salad, but I feel like eating the fries. Result? Fries 1, Salad 0.

It is very easy for the Physical State Pillar to be ignored altogether, until you fall sick or injured, of course! As we have already seen, rebuilding the capacity to pay attention to your body and your Physical State Pillar can be very powerful, and nowhere is this more true than with nutrition.

Food and Resistance

For so many people, food choices and their nutrition have become a painful issue, full of resistance, frustration and guilt. They go through the week resisting "X" because they know they should not eat "X". But by focussing on not eating "X", the picture of "X" just becomes bigger and juicier in their mind, until in the end, often during the weekend, when they are tired or late at night, their willpower breaks down and they quickly shovel down a huge amount of "X". The result is that they feel guilty, and make a promise to themselves never to eat "X" again, and the whole cycle repeats!

The more you resist something, the more it grows and the more you are inexorably drawn towards it: your mind does not process the negative—If I tell you to *not* think of ice cream, then what happens? It is a veritable ice cream parlour in your mind right now. By focussing on what you have decided you should not be eating, you make it more likely that you end up eating it! This is why finding nutritious foods to *add* to your diet is generally a more effective approach than trying to *remove* unhealthy ones.

Emotional Motivation

Although we would like to think that we are supremely rational in our choices, it is the emotional factors that often dictate our actions (remember "e-motion": "that which puts us into action"). You probably already know what you *should* eat; it is just that most of the time you are simply not doing what you know you should! There is, therefore, little point in this book trotting out the same old tired clichés, giving you the same information that you have already ignored many times before!

Awareness versus Advice

Although there will be the odd piece of advice thrown in, the focus of this section is really the same as the rest of the book for us: to introduce the key distinctions, for you to pay attention to your current habits and then to see if they are "working" for you—what I mean by "working" is this:

If you keep doing it, will you achieve your objective?

You may think your nutrition is "fine", but what do your results say? With regard to nutrition, you basically carry your results around with you every day. So, if you want to be honest about your current situation, then go and stand buck naked in front of a mirror and look closely at what you see. You may not want to do that, but your results are there whether you want to see them or not.

Of course, nutritional habits do not just affect how you look and what you can see in the mirror. When was the last time you had a medical? Were you too busy or too scared of what you might find out? Do you actually know your current cholesterol level, your blood pressure, your triglyceride level or your other key indicators?

The focus of this section will be to look at nutrition through some of the lenses that we have already applied elsewhere in this book. This is not a "healthy eating" or a "diet" book. This is a book aimed at people who take their personal and leadership development seriously and want to optimise the functioning of their whole system in order to deliver peak performance in pursuit of their objective. If you ignore your Physical State Pillar and your nutrition, then you are seriously compromising your ability to produce the results that you dream of creating.

THE SCIENCE

The first thing to get clear on is the physiological necessity of food and drink: without it, we die; it is as simple as that. Every function that your body carries out, internally (such as cell replenishment) and externally (such as lifting your arm) requires energy. The external actions are the ones we often think about as they are the most obvious to us, but stop for a moment and think of everything going on *inside* your body, all the systems that require energy and replenishment if they are to continue to do their essential work:

- nervous system
- circulatory system
- immune system
- respiratory system
- digestive system
- endocrine system
- reproductive system
- urinary system
- skeletal system
- muscular system

All these systems are silently whirring away in the background, doing their job, even as you read this book.

Your Mental and Emotional State Pillars may be in tip-top shape, but if your Physical State Pillar is compromised, then everything suffers. However, despite that, the majority of people with whom I work spend far more time thinking about what they will put *on* their body, rather than *in* it. Clothes seem to matter a lot more to most people today than their nutrition.

Nutrients

Simply put, the food we ingest is broken down into nutrients. There are macronutrients: proteins (which become amino acids), carbohydrates (which become glucose) and fats (which become fatty acids). All three of these are essential for a healthy functioning body and an effective physical state:

- **Proteins:** facilitate growth, repair of body tissue, regulation of hormones and protection of immune system.
- **Carbohydrates:** provide energy to the brain and the nervous system. Note that there are three types of carbohydrates: sugar, starch (rice, potatoes, pasta, etc.) and fibre (vegetables, fruits, whole grains, etc.).
- **Fats:** provide insulation and energy, protect organs and contribute to brain development and nerve function.

In addition, there are also micronutrients: vitamins, minerals water and phytonutrients. However:

> *"People eat food, not nutrients!"*
> - Krista Scott-Dixon, Precision Nutrition

Food and Your Body

In order for your body to make use of the necessary nutrients from the food you eat, the food first needs to be digested, absorbed and transported around the body. The process begins when you chew the food in your mouth, after which the food enters your stomach where it is further broken down and the nutrients are extracted. From there, the nutrients travel to the small intestine, and with the exception of most fats, they are then directly transported to your body's very own bodyguard: the liver. The liver then carries out a screening process and "decides" what goes where: most notably to the brain (processing usage), the muscles (energy usage) or to fat (energy storage).

When you eat a typical meal, the nutrients take a few hours before they start getting circulated in your blood. The complete digestive process, from ingestion to excretion, can take anywhere from 12 hours to three days.

The brain requires glucose as an energy source, but smart as it may be, it cannot store its own glucose. Therefore, it requires a steady supply if it is to function effectively.

Well, that's really it for the science! I wanted to get you off "automatic mode" with regard to nutrition, to get you to stop and consider, for just a moment, the importance of these everyday activities called eating and drinking. You eat and drink so regularly that your habits in this area become transparent. In fact, it is not usually the habits themselves that become transparent, but rather your stories of justification that support these habits (for example, you might already be aware that you drink six cups of coffee a day but you have lost sight of your justification that you only do it because of your job. And so you think it is OK and there is no need, or even possibility, to do anything different). Once the justification becomes transparent in this way, you are doomed to repeat the same action over and over again, thereby ensuring the same predictable results.

19

EATING HABITS

For those of us lucky enough to be surrounded by plentiful, edible and affordable food, the whole process of eating has either turned into a necessary evil that interrupts what you were doing before you became hungry (a stolen 15 minutes at your desk before you go into another meeting), or else an excuse to indulge and relieve stress (a feast of overindulgence). Many of my coaching clients yo-yo between these two extremes.

Because of their strong connection to our Emotional State Pillar, eating habits can be hard to see and even harder to shift than our other habits, such as walking and breathing. For example, so many of our eating habits go back to our childhood and feelings of connection to our parents, the place (country, town, etc.) we grew up in and nostalgia for simpler and safer times gone by. Equally, food can be a great source of pleasure (and our old friend *comfort*) in the immediate present.

It would be naïve to think that you will ever make 100% of your eating choices according to your body's nutrient requirements. That is simply not going to happen. Even when Sari was taking part in fitness physique championships across Southeast Asia, she did not eat purely according to her physical requirements.

PERSONAL REFLECTION

Sari: Eating Habits

The nutritional requirements for fitness competitions are brutal. There is no way around it. Champions are not made in the gym; they are made in the kitchen.

To make things worse, there are thousands of opinions about what you should eat and when in the three months leading up to a competition: protein, red meat, white meat, fish from the sea, fish from a farm, fish from a river, fats, carbohydrates, starchy carbs, cruciferous carbs, salt, water, vitamins, supplements, high glycemic, low glycemic... Arrgghhh! All of this added to the pressure of leading up to a competition and working harder in the gym than I had ever worked before! In retrospect, however, two things really stand out.

Firstly, the received wisdom is only useful as a starting point. There is no point obsessing about the latest research on salt intake and water retention, if you do not pay attention to how salt is affecting *you*! The theory is just that: theory. Champions do not pay attention to *theory*; they pay attention to how the theory applies to them and their body. For example, I noticed early on that salt and water retention was not such a big thing for me. Although the science and the theory was interesting, it was a distraction for me. There were other things that made more of a difference to my performance. However, based on results, I knew that my body was very sensitive to carbohydrate intake, and focussing on this area made a huge impact.

Secondly, even when competing in a fitness competition, there is no way in the world that I will be able to make purely rational food choices for three whole months. It is just not going to happen. Even in the middle of competition preparation, I am still going to make some emotional and hormonal food decisions. My weakness is bread—I love bagels and bread pudding! When I started out, I felt very guilty about chowing down on bread while preparing for the competition, but as I gained experience, I learned to respect the needs of my body and *my emotions* and trusted that I would not sabotage my purpose.

The killer was not eating the bread;
the killer was feeling guilty about the bread.

If I went to the gym the next day feeling guilty and imagining that my trainer could see the bagel on my hips (oh, the shame!), then everything would collapse and I would set up a vicious cycle where I was more likely to go off track again the next day.

However, if I ate the bread and used it positively the next day in the gym, then it actually worked *for* me, instead of *against* me! Let's look at how this works in the three Internal Pillars:

- **Mental State Pillar:** I am choosing to eat this bread for a reason.
- **Emotional State Pillar:** I am enjoying the experience of eating this bread.
- **Physical State Pillar:** My body needs this nutrient to recover from my recent training session and to prepare for tomorrow's session.

These two factors made a huge impression on me, and I now use them in all my coaching, whatever the subject:

1. The theory is just that—theory. Pay attention to how things are working for *you*!
2. Feeling guilty is a killer which just keeps you stuck in your current cycle. What's done is done. That decision is already gone. What matters now is how you choose to relate to that choice. Guilt is a luxury that you cannot afford if you want to become a champion!

In short, there are physiological reasons why we need food, (Physical State Pillar), but there are also psychological and emotional reasons why we eat (Mental and Emotional State Pillars), and to try and eliminate any one of these will likely leave you in a frustrated mess.

COMFORT & SPEED MATRIX REVISITED

As briefly mentioned in Chapter 16, food and eating patterns also create comfort and discomfort, depending on our eating speed. Let's take another look at the Comfort & Speed Matrix (see Figure 19.1):

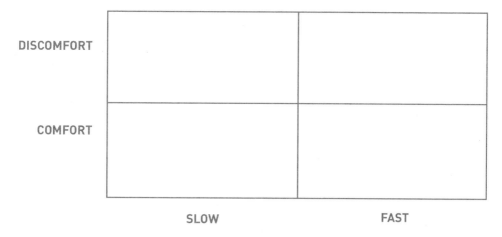

	SLOW	FAST
DISCOMFORT		
COMFORT		

Figure 19.1 Comfort & Speed Matrix

Consider the speed of your food intake and how it impacts your comfort level. As we saw earlier in Chapter 16, the fast and comfortable zone is very popular today; this is the zone where fast food, sugary treats, soda and foods with high glycemic loads live. This is the zone of immediate gratification. Feel hungry, eat fast-acting foods and move on. Rinse and repeat. Even meals eaten at home are often shovelled down as fast as possible so that you can get back to your iPad or your emails.

For many people, food has become a short-term fix for a longer-term issue. All the physiological reasons have been ignored and overridden by the psychological craving for immediate satisfaction or the emotional craving for comfort. However, what begins as fast and comfortable very often ends up becoming uncomfortable when you develop indigestion and acid reflux.

You might remember when we discussed breathing in Chapter 17 that the process of exhaling engages the parasympathetic nervous system and the "rest and *digest*" system. It is not an accident that digestion issues (and the companion industry of digestion medicines) continue to increase exponentially. If you don't make time to "rest and digest", then your Physical State Pillar will eventually make known its displeasure and cause you distress! Despite this, many people continue to take the fast and comfortable route, reasoning that popping a pill later will do the trick.

What do you notice about your own eating patterns? Which zones do *your* eating occasions tend to fall into?

SPEED EATING

I am not a big fan of tips but here is one: if, after reading this chapter, you do nothing else except this one thing, and you do it consistently, then you will notice a big shift, not only in your experience of food, but also in your weight and body composition.

Slow down the pace of your eating!

Ensure that every bite is properly chewed and swallowed, before the next mouthful is started. In Chapter 17, Sari outlined the power of *conscious* movement. The same principle applies here: *conscious* eating. I have worked with people on many practices in this area: timing their meals, getting them to put down their knife and fork or chopsticks between every mouthful or even putting them in the opposite hands, anything that breaks up the unthinking pattern that allows them to blast through their meal at their usual, unthinking, unconscious pace.

Once you slow down your eating, you can actually focus on savouring the food, becoming aware of the tastes and textures that you had lost sight of in your quest to finish your meal as soon as possible. This is a process that very often, in itself, leads to better quality food choices in the future. It is amazing that when you slow down your eating and really pay attention to your experience of what you are consuming, you realise you don't really enjoy many of the foods and drinks that you thought you liked! This is especially true for soda drinkers, who very often cannot even finish one can of their favourite soda when they take time to actually notice the taste and their experience of drinking it!

So many issues with food occur because of fast, unconscious eating. Speed eating not only messes with your digestive system, but it also tends to lead to overeating. By the time you realise you are full, you have already eaten a whole lot more than your body actually needs! Your ability to eat quickly outpaces your body's ability to give you feedback regarding when you are full and can stop. Left to its own devices, the Emotional State Pillar (often in the desire for comfort) drives you to eat far more than your Physical State Pillar requires. However, nowadays, paying attention to the needs of your Physical State Pillar is not as popular (or as practised) as listening to your Emotional State Pillar.

My mother had a useful philosophy in this regard: the next time you think you are hungry, drink a glass of water. If you still feel hungry after drinking the water, then ask yourself if you want an apple. If you do not want an apple, then you are most likely not physically hungry at all. Instead, it is likely that your Emotional or Mental State Pillar is telling you that you need food to soothe some other symptom.

Food addictions and compulsive eating habits tend to be accompanied by fast eating. It is almost as though you are saying to yourself, "If I eat this whole packet of biscuits quickly enough, then my body will not notice the calories." Unfortunately, not only does your body notice the massive calorie influx and store the excess calories as fat, it also pays you back later with digestive issues!

Developing the capacity to stop eating when you feel there is still a little room left is another great habit to practise, but you only have a hope of doing that if you *slow down*!

FOOD AS A QUICK FIX

Sometimes, the speed of your eating is determined by time: for example, you are rushing between meetings or appointments. But very often the speed is necessary because you are experiencing discomfort in another area of your life and you just need a " quick fix" as a distraction. You have a problem with your wife/husband/boss/children and chug down a brownie and a Coke because that instant sugar rush feels mighty good—certainly better than actually handling the issue of your discomfort at its root cause. Then, because you do not handle the root cause, the issue gets worse, and now you need *two* brownies and a shot of rum in that Coke! And the best thing of all? You can justify that behaviour by blaming it all on your wife/husband/boss/children, and so when you get fat or sick, it is *their* fault! How convenient. However, it is *you* who is suffering the consequences of *your* choices!

20

BODY TYPES

There is no one ideal diet that suits everyone, just as there is no one exercise regimen that suits everyone. Different people react differently to the same food. A classic example is caffeine: some people are highly sensitive to it and some are not. This can also change according to age. Throughout this book we stress the importance of remaining conscious, rather than defaulting to automatic, comfortable habits.

With regard to your Physical State Pillar, it is important to become conscious of your body type because it has a significant impact on how your body reacts to different exercises and macronutrient ratios, carbohydrates in particular. In this book, our discussion on body types will primarily focus on how they relate to nutrition rather than physical training. If you are interested in training for your body type, there are many resources on the internet for you to tailor your workout regimen. However, eating according to your body type will help you achieve peak performance not only in your Physical State Pillar, but in your Emotional and Mental State Pillars as well.

There are essentially three body types: the ectomorph, mesomorph and endomorph (see Figure 20.1):

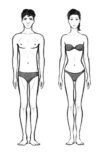 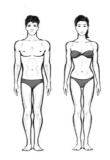 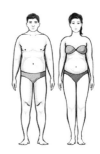

Ectomorph (I Type)   Mesomorph (V Type)   Endomorph (O Type)

Figure 20.1 Body Types[11]

ECTOMORPH (I TYPE)

This body type has a light and lean build, and finds it hard to gain muscle because of a fast metabolism. Ectomorphs tend to be narrow and vertical in appearance. This is my own body type.

MESOMORPH (V TYPE)

This body type has a naturally athletic physique, and finds it easy to gain muscle while staying lean. Mesomorphs tend to have solid, V-shaped frames. This is Sari's body type.

---

11   Berardi, John, et al. *The Essentials of Sport and Exercise Nutrition*. 3rd ed., Precision Nutrition. 2016.

ENDOMORPH (O TYPE)

This body type is more solid and generally soft, and gains fat most easily out of the three body types. Appearance-wise, endomorphs tend to have shorter and rounder frames, with thick arms and legs.

Identifying your body type is a useful initial indicator on how to adjust your nutritional intake and your exercise regimen, but it is not exact and certainly should not be taken as a lifetime genetic guarantee for being slim (ectomorph), muscular (mesomorph) or fat (endomorph). If you are clear on your purpose in your Mental State Pillar, emotionally connected to it in your Emotional State Pillar and aware of your body type in your Physical State Pillar, then you are in a good position to make progress and achieve the body composition that you say you want.

PERSONAL REFLECTION

Marcus: The Ectomorph

When I started working out, I had a very clear purpose to which I was powerfully emotionally connected: to lose weight (as I shared in Chapter 12). I was about to marry Sari and I didn't want to look so horribly out of shape next to her! Back then, Sari was living in Indonesia and I was living in Hong Kong, so I used to carry a little photo of her in my kitbag to ensure I had a constant reminder of my purpose with me whenever I was about to work out. Keep your emotional connection close!

Once I started, it didn't take me long to realise that I needed a personal trainer to prevent me from killing myself (thank you, Ines!). My trainer kept me safe and also introduced me to some new distinctions to which I was blind at the time: losing fat rather than losing weight, for example. Having an expert watch me and introduce new distinctions helped me immeasurably. Something to pay attention to in your own journey is whether you are willing to develop your Support Pillar and grant someone else permission to teach you. It can make a big difference to your results.

With help from my trainer Ines, I began to make quick progress; I lost 18 kg in six months and my enthusiasm began to grow even more. I began to explore for myself and discovered many new distinctions, especially with regard to nutrition and body type. Not unlike many guys who start working out, I soon discovered the urge to pack on some muscle. Given that I had lost so much weight so quickly, I presumed that I would be able to pack on the muscle just as quickly, right? Wrong, very wrong. I soon became frustrated that it just was not happening.

Discovering the distinction between body types was very useful for me. I discovered that I was an ectomorph. This was not a death sentence for the dream of putting on muscle, but it did mean that if I wanted to achieve it, I would have to make some serious adjustments to my workouts and my nutrition. Most notably, I would have to do less cardio, lift more and heavier weights, and eat a *lot more food* (carbohydrates in particular). I did this for a short while, but I hated it. My Emotional State Pillar was just not engaged; I was not emotionally connected to the purpose of having big, bulging muscles. Sure, it was a nice idea, but it did not light my fire in the same way that looking slim next to my new wife did.

Knowing that I am an ectomorph does not make me a prisoner of my body type. Rather, recognising the distinction in my Mental State Pillar has made me more aware of my Physical State Pillar, which has helped me make informed choices about how to progress. Knowing these facts has also affected my Emotional State Pillar by reducing my frustration at making such slow progress, and helped me clarify and refocus on my deeper purpose. It is perfectly possible for an ectomorph to pack on muscle, but it is naïve to pretend that the same exercise and nutrition routine will work both for me and someone with a different body type (and maybe with a very different purpose too).

To this day Ines still calls me "Stick"; I never did make it to "Trunk", but I am not disappointed about that. I discovered what it would take for me to achieve it, and chose something else instead—something I really cared about.

In unrelated news, my favourite animal is the giraffe.

PERSONAL REFLECTION

Sari: The Mesomorph

My journey with food and nutrition has been long and varied. Before I developed an interest in the area of health, fitness and nutrition, I really just ate whatever I wanted without thinking about it, and to many of my friends' envy, I never seemed to put on any weight. What I didn't know then was that I was the classic "skinny fat" person: I actually had a relatively high amount of body fat, which was only hidden by the fact that I had very little muscle mass.

This became very clear when I started to work out, because I immediately realised that I was very weak and lacking in endurance. So, although I appeared "healthy" to many people, this was far from the truth. In actual fact, I was just thin and weak. This really woke me up to how the world at large often defines "healthy" in a purely visual way. When I started to work out, I was thin, not healthy, and they are not the same thing!

As I began to work out, I increased the volume of what I was eating, and in true mesomorph fashion, I began to put on muscle and lose fat. Once again, my friends were envious!

However, it did not take long before I fell into the classic mesomorph trap: because it appeared that I could eat pretty much whatever I liked without fear of getting fat, I just kept eating! Eventually, I went too far, and although I was exercising very hard, my fat content began to increase again, and when I began taking part in fitness competitions, this became a major issue that I needed to work on.

I have learned a great lesson in this journey. I have been blessed with some great genes (I love that I am a mesomorph!), but it means nothing unless I am willing to work hard on my body. My body does seem to have a genetic predisposition to put on muscle, but unless I am disciplined and stay connected to my purpose, I could easily end up becoming overweight. I use this learning all the time with my clients: yes, it is true that we all have a genetic make-up, but it is also true that we all create our bodies and our energy levels through the actions that we take (or do not take). The three body types, while a little simplistic, do provide a great starting point for a conversation about this lesson.

We have been very fortunate to have my nutrition coach Krista Scott-Dixon share her experience as an endomorph for this book. Krista is Director of Curriculum at Precision Nutrition.

PERSONAL REFLECTION

Krista: The Endomorph

I am an endomorph. I come from a family of endomorphs. We are all short and sturdy, low to the ground and solid. Some of us are round and some of us are more teardrop-shaped. What we all have in common is that we will never, ever, barring some horrible disease, be considered "long and lean". All of us have struggled with our weight and size, with varying degrees of success. Body fat seems to find us like a homing pigeon. Genetic testing tells me that I carry some so-called "obesity genes": these are genes that code for things like appetite, body weight and body fatness. They may make my "shut-off switch" of satiety harder to hear, and if I do hear it, they make me more likely to just happily blast right past it.

A classic endomorph is built to store fat; you won't believe it, but this was once a good thing. During the ice age when food was scarce, endomorphs were more likely than ectomorphs to survive the harsh conditions. But it's a different story now, when food is readily available.

For a long time, I thought I was doomed by my genetic heritage. I never went through a "coltish" phase as many girls do, all legs and arms and impossibly slim hips. Instead, I seemed to go straight from "shortest kid in the class" to "shortest, stumpiest teenager in the class".

When endomorphs go on a diet, as most of us inevitably do in a futile attempt to look like magazine people or simply feel "normal" in a culture that values thinness and six-pack abs, our metabolic rate downshifts more than average. We may lose up to 10 to 15 percent of our normal metabolic "idling speed" when we restrict our calorie intake, especially if we really go at it hard. This means if we normally expended 2000 calories a day, now we may expend 1700 to 1800 calories. Which means we have to eat *even less*, and exercise *even more*. And unlike ectomorphs (the skinny spider people), we don't tend to compensate for extra energy coming in. If you feed an ectomorph more than they need, their body will turn up the thermostat, and they are likely to expend extra energy as heat. We endomorphs, however, will likely store whatever extra energy you give us. After all, another ice age could happen after lunch!

Nearly 30 years ago, I discovered the weight room and discovered that female bodybuilders were "a thing". I lifted weights on and off until I finally committed to it 20 years ago.

Since then, I've missed few workouts. My body has changed. My metabolism has changed. And so has my perspective.

I discovered that we are not "doomed" at all.
I discovered that activity and movement change the game.
Fitting your activity to your body changes the game.
Awareness changes the game.

As an endomorph, I discovered that hitting the gym and lifting weights worked! My awareness changed my activity and my new activity changed my nutrition choices. Protein, and lots of it, worked wonders for me. Raw vegetables? Not so much, thankfully! I also noticed that when I started exercising and moving, my body handled carbohydrates so much better, compared to when I had been sedentary. Suddenly, I could eat some carbohydrates without it sticking to me! Now, I can enjoy that post-workout pasta or potato, knowing that when I eat those carbohydrates after I have worked hard, they will do their proper job of refuelling my strength and vitality. I learned that:

When I am fit and consistently active,
my body knows what to do with the carbohydrates I eat.

My key learning over the years has been this:

The more I move, the better my body will work.

This is true of all body types, of course. But it is particularly important for endomorphs, who get the worst of all worlds if we are sedentary: excess body fat plus excess body weight plus little muscle to offset it, which adds up to having to drag around a big bag of body fat with no engine to do it. If we are active, we will still be bigger but we will also be stronger, fitter, more powerful, and perhaps most importantly, metabolically healthy.

As an endomorph, I *can* lose body fat, but in all likelihood, I will never be as ripped as my ectomorph friends. I am heavier than average, edging into the official "overweight" category by Body Mass Index, but I am also leaner than average. For some years, I walked around at about 15 to 17 percent body fat, something very unusual for a female endomorph, simply thanks to good nutrition and regular exercise. These days I cruise around 21 percent, which is more comfortable to maintain in my 40s.

If you are thoughtful and wise about what you eat, how you eat and how much you eat, and you honour your appetite with conscious eating, enjoying the sensuous pleasure of food while not eating too much, you can easily maintain your strength along with a healthy, vibrant body weight and body fat level.

In these reflections, each of us talks about experiences common to our respective body types. Making conscious choices based on an awareness of your body type is an important first step in optimising your physical performance. As we have already seen many times, the physical, mental and emotional states are highly interlinked, making nutrition a key factor in your overall performance.

MACRONUTRIENT GUIDELINES BY BODY TYPE

Nutritionally, each body type processes food differently. This is particularly true when it comes to carbohydrates, which ectomorphs tend to process a lot more efficiently and effectively than endomorphs do. This factor means that the recommended optimal macronutrient split is rather different across the three body types. In Figure 20.2, Krista has kindly provided some guidelines when it comes to working out the macronutrient ratio for the your body type.

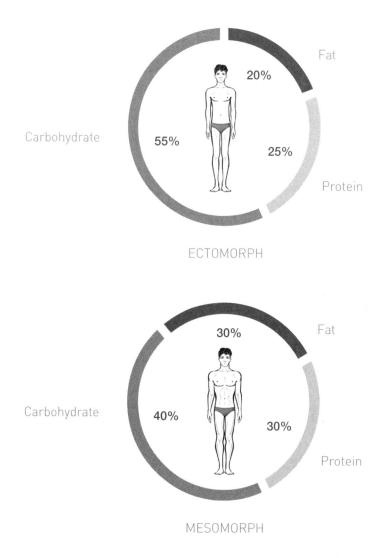

Fat

20%

Carbohydrate   55%   25%

Protein

ECTOMORPH

Fat

30%

Carbohydrate   40%   30%

Protein

MESOMORPH

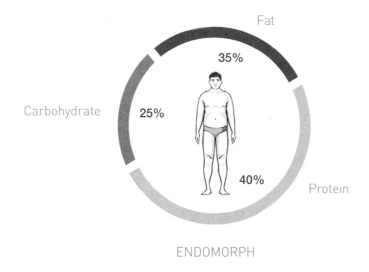

Fat

35%

Carbohydrate   25%

40%

Protein

ENDOMORPH

Figure 20.2 Precision Nutrition Macronutrient Guidelines for Each Body Type

Even though we are looking at the issue at a rather simplistic level here, you can immediately see the madness of looking for the one perfect diet or exercise plan, following the latest food fads or even the workout plan that your favourite celebrity uses, especially if your favourite celebrity has a completely different body type from yours. When it comes to exercise and nutrition, there is no "one-size-fits-all" solution. The secret is that there is no secret. Instead, what works is to become conscious of your own personal starting point with regard to your Physical, Mental and Emotional State Pillars and then to tailor your actions in pursuit of a purpose to which you are emotionally connected. Remember that the information provided in this chapter is just a set of *guidelines*. Pay attention to your results and adjust accordingly.

21

CONSCIOUS EATING

When considering nutrition, people generally spend most of their time thinking (or even obsessing!) about what they should or should not eat. However, *how* you eat and *how much* you eat are also at least as important. You can make all the "right" choices when it comes to *what* you eat, but if you are consistently eating portions that are too big or too small, then you are not going to produce the results that you seek. The difficulty is that no one has the patience to measure out grams or calculate calories all day long, and so they just eat until they feel full. As we saw earlier, the problem is that by the time you realise you are full, you have already eaten more than you need because of the time lag between putting something in your mouth and your body telling you that it is satisfied. The faster you eat, the higher risk you have of overeating.

Fortunately, your body can help you out with regard to portion control. You are already carrying around perfect measuring units for the key macronutrients in your diet: your hands! Once again, I am indebted to Krista Scott-Dixon and Precision Nutrition for this helpful guide.

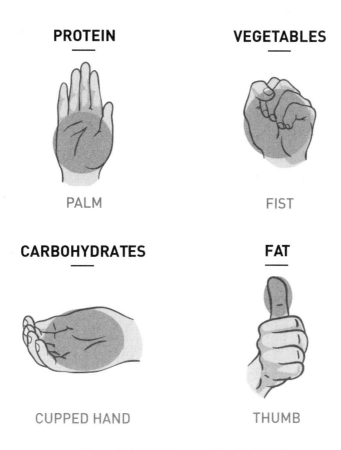

PROTEIN

PALM

VEGETABLES

FIST

CARBOHYDRATES

CUPPED HAND

FAT

THUMB

Figure 21.1 Hand-Measured Portion Guide[12]

---

12 These images are from Precision Nutrition's guide to calorie control at
    www.precisionnutrition.com/calorie-control-guide-infographic.

To review:

- Your palm determines your protein portions. A palm-sized portion should be the same thickness and diameter as your palm.
- Your fist determines your vegetable portions. As with your protein portions, a fist-sized portion should be the same thickness and diameter as your fist.
- Your cupped hand determines your carbohydrate portions. This is slightly different: one carbohydrate portion should fit inside your cupped hand.
- Your thumb determines your fat portions. A thumb-sized portion should be the same thickness and diameter as your thumb.

This is a simple and effective way to start monitoring your portion sizes. Men can work on the basis that two palms of protein, two fists of vegetables, two cupped hands of carbohydrates and two thumbs of fat are appropriate amounts for each meal. Women can work on the basis that one palm of protein, one fist of vegetables, one cupped hand of carbohydrates and one thumb of fat are appropriate amounts for each meal.

Now, this is not a perfect, one-size-fits-all system. In fact, you might have noticed that it can contradict the macronutrient guidelines I have provided for each body type in Chapter 20. It is, however, an excellent (and convenient!) starting point for most people. Of course, as you become more advanced in your nutritional planning, you can begin to adjust for factors such as body type and other requirements.[13] For example, a typical male endomorph might start with three thumbs of fat-dense foods and only one cupped handful of carbohydrates and work from there. However, if you begin by using this system for portion control, paying attention to the results that it creates for you, and then adjusting accordingly, you are on your way.

Most people I know who have tried this system initially feel that their portions are too small because their prior habit has been to quickly and unthinkingly eat until either they feel physically full, or the emotional or mental issue that was driving them to eat has been silenced. However, if you

---

13   Precision Nutrition has further modified this portion control guide to fit each body type at
      http://www.precisionnutrition.com/all-about-body-type-eating.

combine these portion size recommendations with the recommendations to slow down the speed of your eating, and to pay attention to your experience of the eating process, then will you soon become accustomed to the new portion size.

If you are serious about your nutrition and performance,
then looking at what *you eat is only a part of the story;*
be prepared to pay at least as much attention to
how *you eat and* how much *you eat.*

FOOD AND ENERGY

One of the primary physiological needs for food is to produce energy. In most circumstances, a steady flow of glucose moving around your system at all times is effective—this is the blood sugar level that you might have read about. The advantage of keeping your blood sugar level steady is that by avoiding peaks and troughs throughout the day, you not only keep a steady supply of energy coursing through your system, you also avoid the desire to snack on cookies and cake mid-morning and mid-afternoon. That is why you might have heard of the concept of eating regularly and often throughout the day: three main meals, supplemented by healthy snacks (containing protein) in between, as well as a protein snack before bedtime. For most people, this is a good solid, basic system (good snacks include nuts and fruit), but as stated above, if it is not working for you, then change it up.

Again, remaining *conscious* is what works. What worked for you in the past may no longer be working for you in the present. As with exercise, your body is quick to adapt to patterns, and the impact of your past meal plans can quickly be diminished. That is why some people advocate calorie cycling (with high-calorie and low-calorie days) and intermittent fasting. The desire for a familiar, comfortable life is very strong, especially when it comes to making food choices, so being willing to consciously shift your patterns is a powerful habit to cultivate.

WILLPOWER

People often praise Sari and me for our "amazing willpower" when it comes to nutrition. Nothing could be further from the truth. I am very partial to chocolate cake (see Appendix I), and Sari has mentioned her love for bagels and bread pudding. However, whenever we go "off-plan" we do it consciously, and we certainly do not feel guilty about it when we do. If you want the burger, have the burger, enjoy it (or, if you take your time to eat it, you might notice that you actually do not enjoy it), and then pay attention to your next food choice. If you are clear in your purpose (Mental State Pillar) and you are emotionally connected to it (Emotional State Pillar), then you will find a way to balance out your choices, especially if you remain conscious of what your body (Physical State Pillar) is telling you that it needs.

The other thing that really works in this area is being a *conscious shopper*. Shopping when you're bored, hungry or tired can lead you to buy things that are not in line with your purpose. You do not need willpower to avoid eating the biscuits if they are not in your cupboard in the first place! Remember:

If you don't buy it, then you cannot eat it!

LISTENING TO YOUR BODY

As with the other sections in this book, there is no one secret solution. What works is remaining *conscious* of your choices, paying attention to your current results and using them as a guide for your future action. There is no miracle food. If you are heavier or lighter than you say you want to be, then you need to make different choices with regard to your movement and/or your nutrition. Whether you make those new choices or not will depend on how emotionally connected you are to your purpose.

As with exercise, the problem that most people face with nutrition is that to be on point, it helps if you are willing to go against many of the 21st-century trends by doing the following:

- slowing down your eating, instead of rushing through your meals.
- thinking ahead and preparing food, instead of just eating what is immediately and conveniently available.
- paying attention to the needs of your Physical State Pillar and listening to your body, instead of simply listening to your Emotional State Pillar and its desire for immediate gratification and comfort.
- staying *conscious* in the moment of eating, rather than mindlessly shoveling in food and drink while you watch TV, read emails, chatter away, text or surf the web.

Learning to listen to your body and being able to distinguish the needs of your Physical State Pillar from the needs of your Mental or Emotional State Pillars is a journey. It requires practice. It is a practice in itself. It does not happen immediately. It is also not a science and so there is no profit in becoming lost in an endless introspection of whether something is a message from your physical or emotional state.

However, if you are willing to persevere, then you will notice that listening to your body and paying attention to your Physical State Pillar can play a huge role in your personal and leadership development, because it influences everything about you—how you think, how you feel, and ultimately therefore what you do. If you are willing to do this and to identify a purpose to which you are emotionally connected, then you will notice a marked shift in your nutritional habits. This shift will be far more pronounced than that created by reading more and more information about what you should or should not eat.

**PART II:
SELF-REFLECTION**

It is time to review what you have discovered about yourself while reading Part II. Again, answer these questions as honestly as you can so that you know where you are right now in terms of your body and nutrition.

DEFINING FITNESS

1. My definition of fitness is:

2. My definition of physical health is:

3. On a scale of 1 to 10 (1 being the lowest, 10 being the highest), my level of physical health is:

4. The criteria I use to assess my physical health are:

5. I believe that the factors preventing my physical health from being a 10 are:

6. I believe that the factors that go into creating and maintaining a healthy relationship with somebody are:

7. I create effective relationships with people when I am willing to:

Now, consider this idea:

> *Your physical health is a relationship between you and your body.*

Take another look at the list and compare your relationships with people to your relationship with your body. If you treated your best friend in the same way that you treat your body, would they still be your best friend? If you treated your husband or wife in the same way, would you still be married?

POSTURE AND FORM

Now reflect on your posture and form. There are two easy ways to do this:

a. Looking into the mirror, stand or sit normally, and write down what you see.
b. Ask a trusted friend to stand in front of you and to "mirror" your body posture. Then tell them to exaggerate it.

Once you have done one or both of these, note down what you have become aware of and the likely consequences.

1. What I have realised about my posture is:

2. The likely physical, mental and emotional consequences of these are:

EXERCISE

Let's turn to your relationship with exercise.

1. My definition of exercise is:

2. My experience of exercise is:

3. My favourite excuses for not exercising are:

What do you notice about your answers? Remember, in this part we looked at how exercise does not only help your body function more effectively, it can also make you smarter! I hope your excuses are really worth it!

HABITS

Make a list of some of your habits (under the emotional, mental and physical domains), and then imagine the consequences if you continue to let them run through your life unchecked. Remember that habits are things that you do consistently, whether you like them or not.

1. My physical habits are:

2. If I keep these habits throughout my life, I imagine that I will:

3. My mental habits are:

4. If I keep these habits throughout my life, I imagine that I will:

5. My emotional habits are:

6. If I keep these habits throughout my life, I imagine that I will:

STRESS

Consider the levels of stress that you typically experience in the various areas of your life.

1. The areas where I typically experience (or have experienced) minimal levels of stress are:

2. The areas where I typically experience (or have experienced) distress are:

3. The areas where I typically experience (or have experienced) eustress are:

What do these various levels of stress tell you about your level of performance in the different areas of your life?

REST AND RECOVERY

Now, let's consider your attitude towards rest and holidays.

1. My opinion of holidays (eg. "Holidays are important", "Taking a break is for wimps") is:

Now look at your actual results regarding holidays. To do this, look back at your past schedule.

2. I took _____ mini-breaks yesterday.
3. Last month, I took _____ days off (and actually relaxed on these days off).
4. In total, I took _____ weeks off from work last year.

Also pay attention to how many hours of sleep you had during the past week. Seven hours of sleep a night is generally considered the absolute minimum if you want to perform at a sustainably high level.

5. On average, I had _____ hours per night during the past week.

Consider whether your *ideas* regarding rest and restoration match up to your actual *results*. Remember, it is your results that matter, not your ideas.

6. When it comes to rest and recovery, I have noticed that:

DISCOMFORT AND COMFORT

Consider all the important elements of your life (family, career, health, etc.) and take a good look at the balance between comfort and discomfort.

1. The areas of my life where discomfort is greater than comfort are:

2. The areas of my life where comfort is greater than discomfort are:

3. What I have noticed about the balance between comfort and discomfort in my life as a whole:

NUTRITION AND YOUR BODY

Stand in front of the mirror and write down what you notice about yourself. Consider your Physical, Emotional and Mental State Pillars as you do this. Where do you feel most uncomfortable. Why?

1. What I notice about myself when I look at my reflection:

Now, think about your primary health indicators (blood pressure, resting heart rate, etc.). If you do not know anything about your primary health indicators, that's something to take note in itself.

2. What I have noticed about my primary health indicators:

FOOD AS A QUICK FIX

Note down any examples where you use food and drink as a way to "medicate" the discomfort you feel in other areas of your life.

1. Some foods that I am using as a way to avoid dealing with other issues in my life are:

2. The areas of my life that I avoid handling by seeking refuge in food are:

BODY TYPES

Based on the information provided in Chapter 20 or using an online test, consider your body type and circle it below.

1. My body type is:
    Ectomorph / Mesomorph / Endomorph

2. The recommended macronutrient split for my estimated body type is:

    Protein: _____%
    Fat: _____%
    Carbohydrate: _____%

Now note down your estimate of your daily macronutrient split. Use the information in Chapter 21 to estimate your portions.

3. My estimated daily macronutrient split is:

Protein: _____%
Fat: _____%
Carbohydrate: _____%

Note: this is an area where people are notoriously inaccurate in their estimations (conveniently "forgetting" that afternoon muffin, for example!). Try taking photos of everything you eat and drink, or using food log apps for a week before you do this exercise again. You will probably get a rather different picture the second time round!

Assess these notes against your purpose and your results. Are your results telling you that something needs to change? If so, then note it down below.

4. What needs to change based on my results:

FROM THE BODY TO LEADERSHIP DEVELOPMENT

This brings the second part of our journey to a close. In it Marcus and I have focussed on two key areas that relate to the body and awareness in the Physical State Pillar: conscious movement and conscious eating. Although we have been concerned with predominantly physical matters in this section, you will notice that the Mental and Emotional State Pillars have constantly emerged as key factors in the equation as well.

Throughout Parts I and II of this book, we have sought to stress the importance of always paying attention to all Five Pillars of Performance in your quest for improved performance, because they are all integrated and fundamental to your effectiveness personally and as a leader. The Five Pillars of Performance serve as a bridge that links these two seemingly separate worlds of personal development and the body. If you can now begin to see these two worlds as fundamentally linked, then a whole new world of possibility opens up for you in your life, and in particular with regards to your leadership.

PART III

LEADERSHIP TRANSFORMED

BY MARCUS & SARI

22

REDEFINING LEADERSHIP

Having looked at the world of personal development in Part I and the world of the body through movement and nutrition in Part II, what remains is to bring them together in Part III, and by so doing create a new way of approaching leadership development, a way that incorporates all Five Pillars of Performance. In particular, this will be an approach that ensures that the Physical State Pillar takes its rightful seat at the table. As a way to begin, we need to return to the subject of leadership and consider a fundamental question: what is it that distinguishes leading from other ways of being?

Here, we offer a very basic definition of leadership, one that we touched on early in Part I: fundamentally, leadership is a *relationship.* It is a relationship where you follow someone else by *choice*, rather than through fear of reprisal or because the other person has one more stripe on their arm than you do. If someone chooses to follow you in pursuit of something you care about when there is no possibility of recrimination or punishment, then you know you have your leadership mojo working!

Viewed in this manner, you can see that leadership is very personal and it shows up *everywhere*, not just in the office. Do your children follow you because you have the title of "parent", or do they choose to follow you because of how you relate to them as a human being? This definition also makes a clear distinction between a leader and "the boss". While the latter uses hierarchy to get the job done, the former uses their way of relating. Of course, the leader may also have hierarchical power; the two terms are not mutually exclusive.

PERSONAL REFLECTION

Marcus: Leaders and Bosses

In my life and my career, I have had bosses who functioned as leaders in my life and bosses who functioned as bosses. My experience in either case was very different.

When I was working with someone I simply saw as a boss, I still worked hard and got the job done as requested, but nothing more. In contrast, when I worked with someone I saw as a leader, it was a totally different experience: by choosing to follow them, it unlocked what I would call my "discretionary energy", a term referring to the energy dedicated to tasks beyond the basic requirements and expectations of a job. With someone I recognised as a leader, I worked hard, got the job done (often exceeding expectations) and enjoyed the experience. The contrast was marked, much like the difference between driving with the handbrake on versus driving full throttle.

Consider the people in your life whom you have *chosen* or are *choosing* to follow, and consider why you are making that choice. When most people do this, they realise that the reasons they choose to follow someone are personal and linked to the qualities of that person. Factors such as the school they went to, the letters after their name and where they were born may have *some* relevance, but they are very rarely the deciding factor. Instead, factors such as integrity, walking the talk, authenticity, passion and a "can-do" attitude tend to be the key elements when it comes to choosing to follow someone. It is incredible when you see that and then consider how much angst people often have about factors such as their university or birthplace!

The challenging leadership question is therefore:

"Why would someone choose to follow you?"

This question forces you to look at yourself and consider how you show up for other human beings in *reality*, not in your mind or in theory, but in day-to-day life.

FEEDBACK: IMPACT INTENDED VERSUS IMPACT FELT

What is the *actual* impact that you have on other people? What happens to other people's Mental, Physical and Emotional State Pillars when you walk into a room? If you really want to take a look at your leadership in this context, then compare the imaginary impact you *intend* to create with the actual impact people *feel* when they are in your presence. Your "impact intended" is easy to identify as it exists in your head. Your "impact felt" is less easy to identify, as it requires other people to be honest with you.

However, if you create the right environment and reassure them that you are sincere in your desire to understand so that you can improve your leadership, then it is very possible to receive honest feedback. When you receive the feedback, it is critical that you just say "thank you" and move on. Any attempt to justify or explain your actions makes the whole exercise pointless. If you are able to obtain an honest picture and accept it as such, then this can make a huge difference to your leadership.

Most of the leaders whom we coach initially have very little idea of the impact they actually have on the people around them; instead they just assume that the impact they intend to create is the impact actually being felt by the people around them. We have facilitated such a conversation many times, and very often the leader is shocked when they hear the honest feedback from the people around them. Of course, this may be hard to hear at the time, but if you are willing to engage openly in this conversation, then ultimately your leadership will benefit greatly in spite of the hits your image might take along the way.

P.E.R.M.: THE FOUR FUNDAMENTALS OF LEADERSHIP

What we offer next is a way of looking at leadership that seeks to expand rather than replace the more established models out there, by giving a fundamental place at the table to your body and the Physical State Pillar. Enter P.E.R.M.: the four fundamentals of leadership.

- Purpose: Why do you want to achieve what you want to achieve?
- Energy: Do you have the energy to achieve it?
- Resilience: Can you keep going in the face of the inevitable obstacles?
- Movement: Are you able to move yourself and others in pursuit of what you want to achieve?

None of these four leadership fundamentals are unique to our model. However, what we aim to offer with this model is an alternative way to approach these fundamentals. Our approach seeks to synthesise a lot of what has gone before and in particular to leverage the power of the Physical State Pillar alongside the more commonly recognised Mental and Emotional State Pillars.

Few would dispute that purpose, energy, resilience and movement are four critical elements in leadership. However, acknowledging their importance is one thing; being able to develop them is another issue altogether. Let's examine and amplify each of these four fundamentals in turn.

23

PURPOSE

In Chapter 7, we saw the power of knowing your purpose, and in particular, how understanding *why* you want what you want is critical if you are to achieve it. It is your emotional connection to your purpose that is the key driving force.

And so it is with leadership. Being in touch with the power of your Emotional State Pillar is critical. *Why* do you want to lead? For what purpose do you want to lead? For the sake of what? If leadership is the "what" that you want to achieve, then you need to be clear on the "why", because consciously or not, it is the "why" that will drive you. Keep drilling down on that question and see where it takes you.

- I want to lead people because:

- And that is important to me because:

- And that is important to me because:

- And that is important to me because:

Keep going until you reach what you experience as the bottom line. There is no right or wrong answer to this question. There is only *your* answer, and that is what is important. *You* need to know what drives *you*. What is the feeling that you say you will experience if you are successful as a leader? Remember that this feeling is not at all linked to being a successful leader: maybe you will succeed as a leader and experience this feeling, or maybe you will succeed as a leader and you will experience something altogether different. On the other hand, maybe you will not succeed as a leader and still experience the feeling you desire anyway, or maybe you will not succeed as a leader, and not experience the feeling. As Marcus has said in Chapter 7, there is no intrinsic link between your tangible goal and the intangible experience that you hope to attain when you achieve it.

LEADER *OF* VERSUS LEADER *FOR*

Over the years, we have it found useful in our coaching to make the distinction between these two ideas:

Being a leader
of something
versus
Being a leader
for something

You might be the leader *of* the team, *of* the company, etc., and that is likely to be a hierarchical distinction. It comes with some kind of title. For example, I am the managing partner and therefore the leader *of* this company. There is nothing wrong with that, but as we saw right at the beginning of this book, being the titular head of the team might make you the *boss*, but it doesn't mean that people will choose to follow you, and hence you might not be a leader as defined in this book.

Being a leader *for* something is entirely different. What are you leading *for*? Another way to look at this is to ask yourself, "What do I stand for? What is it that I am looking to create through and with my leadership?" The answers to questions such as these tend to be deep and value-driven. For example, you might choose to lead for the value of honesty and contribution. If that is the case, then these two things will inform your interactions with the people around you: you speak honestly (even if you fear people will be offended), and you ensure that you are acting for the benefit of others (rather than merely looking after your own interests). Consider the following questions:

- Based on your *results*, what are you currently leading for?
- What do you *want* to lead for?
- What impact do you want to create on other people's Mental, Physical and Emotional State Pillars?

PERSONAL REFLECTION

Sari: Leader *Of* versus Leader *For*

When I first heard of the distinction between being a leader *of* something and being a leader *for* something, it made instant sense to me. There is very little that I can be considered a leader *of*: I am the co-founder of SPI, but that is about it. However, there is much that I have grown to be a leader *for*. This is something that has developed in me over the last few years. As I have taken health, fitness and coaching more seriously, my vision has become clearer and clearer, especially with regard to women. My vision for women is that we all have the power to be strong and flexible without sacrificing any femininity. Women can move with grace and a sense of flow without sacrificing any power.

Women have muscles and curves;
there is no need to hide either of them.

Very often, I work with women who have a well-defined physical state but who are uncertain in their mental and emotional states; they are uncomfortable in their own skin. Sometimes they call it a "body image issue". What I do is to have them consider volunteering to support a cause that they feel connected to. By having an outward-focussed goal, these women often realise that having a six-pack is actually not that important in comparison with being a leader for contribution and empowerment. I love to work with women who want to define who they are in the world without comparing themselves to other women, or to men.

Over time, I have developed and embodied this quality in myself and I have discovered that as I demonstrate this in how I live my life, this draws other women to work with me. Very often, it is not a verbal thing: I don't articulate it to people and they don't say it to me, and yet it is somehow understood between us. It is as though I have a kind of unspoken noticeboard hovering above my head!

So, I am a leader *for* empowered women: for women to develop their strength, their flexibility, their grace to ultimately become women who are happy to be themselves in the world. This is my stand, the purpose to which I am emotionally connected. It is what I choose to lead *for* in the world.

KNOWING THE PURPOSE OF OTHERS

There is another side to this question of purpose. If you want to have people choose to follow you, then it helps if you know what *their* purpose is. What do *they* want to achieve and why do *they* want to achieve it? To what or to whom are they emotionally connected? Attempting to lead without any sense of what exists in someone else's Emotional State Pillar is like driving while wearing a blindfold. Once you know their purpose, then you can build a bridge between your interests and theirs, which immeasurably improves your chances of having them choose to follow you, while at the same time leading for the values that you believe to be important.

We use a simple model that helps you ascertain what it is that different people are looking to create in their lives. In general, there are four big drivers: personal recognition, immediate results, certainty and co-operation. Of course, there are many finer distinctions that can be made, but this broad brush is often a good place to start, especially when you are starting out with a new person or group of people.

However, it is not enough to simply be conscious of your purpose and the purpose of others. There needs to be more than awareness and discovery; there needs to be something that calls the other person into *action*. Something must change with regard to their Physical State Pillar. If they just *feel* different (Emotional State Pillar) or *think* different (Mental State Pillar), then it does not really matter. If a person chooses to follow you but does not put that choice into *action*, then it is of no real consequence. Like many of the factors discussed in this book, leadership only matters when it shows up in the world, in action. A person who chooses to follow you purely in thought and not in action cannot really be said to have chosen to follow you at all.

So, if you aspire to develop as a leader, then not only do you need to be emotionally connected to your own purpose, you also need to be able to unlock the discretionary energy of others by linking your purpose to theirs. This link is often made real and translated into action via a request or an offer.

REQUESTS AND OFFERS

Requests and offers are two more speech acts (remember assertions and assessments from Chapter 5?), and you make them based on your assessment of the future. You make a request of someone when you assess that the future will not turn out the way *you* desire. You make an offer to someone when you assess that the future will not turn out the way that *they* desire. Amongst other things, a good request presupposes that the person to whom it is addressed is competent to fulfil it, whereas a good offer presupposes your own competence to fulfil what you are offering. You make a request of another person in order to enlist their *support* and to help create the future that you desire. This "coalition building" is one of the most important things that leaders do.

One of the things that differentiates a good leader from a great one is their willingness to make both requests *and* offers. A request seeks to enroll support for that to which *you* are emotionally connected while an offer seeks to lend support to that which *someone else* is emotionally connected.

Figure 23.1 Coinciding Visions

Figure 23.1 illustrates this point: An effective leader sees the power in both and is constantly looking for links between what *they* are emotionally connected to and what *other people* are emotionally connected to. In this way, they seek to ensure that their requests coincide with the visions of others and that their offers coincide with their own vision. This creates a win-win situation.

Support is one of the Five Pillars of Performance for this very reason; it is fundamental to effective leadership. The issue of requesting and offering support has come up before in Part I, when we uncovered the way your image can hold you back from achieving the results that you say you want. This is similar ground to when we looked at saying "no". When I am coaching people, these factors are often intertwined and all serve to trap the client in a web of their image's making:

- I don't like to say "no".
- I don't like to ask for support.
- I don't like to make requests and/or offers.

This web is generally spun for the reasons we have already uncovered in Chapter 9: they are trying to be either a "Superhero" or a "Nice Guy/Gal". The fear of losing face in the domain of the Mental State Pillar ("I think I will look incapable if I make a request" or "I think I will mess up if I make an offer") and the Emotional State Pillar ("I will feel embarrassed if I make a request" or "I will feel burdened if I make an offer") makes you less likely to take action in the Physical State Pillar.

The unwillingness to make (big) requests and offers is particularly debilitating in the domain of leadership. If you are unwilling to make requests and offers, then your engagement level with other people is likely to be shallow and your ability to enroll them into action compromised. Without this, your leadership is theoretical at best, a nice concept that exists in your mind.

Requests are interesting things. While they are fundamental to leadership and generally getting things done in life, they are often withheld and when they are withheld, they mutate into expectations. Requests and expectations are two very different things. A good request is clearly communicated in a way that leads to effective action. On the other hand, an expectation simply exists in the mind of the person who wants to see a new future. Although it is never actually communicated, the person who holds the expectation still *expects* the other person to fulfil it, exactly as if they had communicated a request. They essentially expect the other person to be a mind reader, and if the other person's mind-reading fails (as surely it will), then there is hell to pay, because "you should have known to do/not do that"! This is one of the most common breakdowns in leadership and relationships in general.

This unwillingness to take action and communicate requests leads to consequences in the Emotional State Pillar (feelings of frustration, anger and impatience), the Mental State Pillar (thinking that someone is stupid or uncooperative) and the Physical State Pillar (experiencing tension and an increased heart rate).

PERSONAL REFLECTION

Marcus: Requests and Offers

Your willingness (or unwillingness) to make requests and offers is another good example of something that can be traced back to beliefs you formed in your early days of growing up, and as such, it tends to disappear from your view. I remember very clearly my mum telling me when I was growing up, "Those who ask don't get". It was only many years later when I started out in personal development that I began to realise that other people were brought up with the opposite belief: "Those who don't ask don't get"! Up until that point, my assessment was that people who asked for what they wanted were just arrogant and selfish!

This is a very real example of what we were discussing in Part I when we looked at the power of beliefs and assessments in the Mental State Pillar. It is not as though either of these beliefs is true or false, or that one is better than the other; it simply shows how powerful these beliefs are and how a lot of their power derives from their transparency. For as long as I cannot see this kind of belief, I am trapped in an invisible web through which I peer out, experience the world and make my judgements and assessments about myself ("I'm a nice guy"), other people ("he's selfish") and ultimately, the world ("the world is unfair"). As I develop these patterns in my Mental State Pillar, so I develop accompanying patterns in my Emotional State Pillar (feelings of sadness and resentment become common while feelings of gratitude and joy disappear) and my Physical State Pillar (I experience tightness and a closed body position becomes comfortable to me).

Similarly, when I work with my clients, I see that so many of them have carried assessments, such as "I am not good/smart/likeable enough", for a very long time. These long-held assessments hold them back from making the offers that would take their leadership to a whole new level. One of the biggest assessments that I uncovered early on in my own journey of self-awareness was that I held myself back from making offers because I believed that other people could and should do it for themselves. After all, I had grown up with the idea that "those who ask don't get". But this is something that I see mirrored in many of my clients today. What I learned and now work on with my clients is to look underneath such an assessment, because very often what you find is the dislike of the *experience* of making an offer: "If I make the offer to someone else, it makes me vulnerable. What if I then fail and let them down? What if they think that I see myself as superior to them"? Once again, it is all made up! However, such an assessment puts an extremely powerful obstacle in the way of your desire to be an effective leader.

A large part of the power of a personal development journey lies in your ability to uncover beliefs such as these, and see them for what they are—beliefs—and to distinguish them from facts. Facts may be loosely defined as "universal truths which apply to everybody in every situation". On the other hand, a belief is something that, while it may be supported by evidence, is still not universally true. Confusing facts and beliefs is similar to confusing assertions and assessments, and as we saw in Chapter 5, it is a recipe for disaster. "Those who ask don't get" is an example of a belief or an assessment: there is nothing wrong with it, but if I live my life as though it is an assertion or a fact, then I am trapped with no way out.

Demands

While some people hold back on making clear requests and instead live in the murky world of hope and expectation, others go the other extreme and instead of making requests, they make demands. A demand is essentially a request that "cannot" be refused. Of course, theoretically, a request can (almost) *always* be refused, but if the price for that refusal is so high that it becomes untenable to the person on the other end of the request, then essentially you are no longer really making a request of that person, you are making a demand. While there is nothing wrong with demands per se, requests are generally more powerful in the domain of leadership, precisely because they can be refused. But why does the potential of refusal make requests more potent in this domain?

Trusting the "Yes"

Leadership, as we have defined it in this book, involves someone *choosing* to follow you. If someone is really going to choose in a meaningful way, then that choice needs to be made in the presence of a real option to decline. Even more than that, if you want to be able to trust the "yes" that you hear, then you need to know that "no" is a possible choice for that person. Interestingly, 99% of the time in team dynamics workshops that we run, the leader is only too happy to hear "no", and is surprised that people feel scared to say it to them! What they want is honesty, so that they can make the most effective decisions sooner rather than later.

People will be unwilling to be honest with you
if they believe that their Physical, Mental or Emotional State Pillars
will suffer as a result of their honesty.

Leaders who rely on the demand rather than the request do not unlock that discretionary energy in others, and as such tend to forge weaker relationships with those around them. Over the course of history, who are the people who have had the least ability to say "no"? Slaves. Consider how you interact with the people around you. In particular, from whom is it acceptable for you to hear "no", and from whom is it not acceptable to hear "no"?

Once again, rather than answer this based on your thoughts, instead take a look at the world outside you. Who have you not heard a "no" from for a while? Chances are that they are nervous about saying it to you, whatever you may think in your mind! If people around you feel unable to say "no" for whatever reason, then they will say "yes" even if they do not really mean it. This is a disaster for relationships, families and teams.

Nothing breaks trust down faster than a "yes" that is really a "no". The person saying "yes" feels compelled to say it, but has no intention of fulfilling the ensuing promise. The person to whom the "yes" is said assumes that the person saying it is sincere, and so takes them at their word. Then, when the promise is unfulfilled and the agreement is broken, assessments of (un)reliability, (in)competency and (in)sincerity are formed, and trust plummets.

As a leader, if you notice that this is happening around you, the fact that people feel compelled to say "yes" to you can be seen as powerful feedback and an important place to intervene. Trust is the lifeblood of relationships (and leadership, as we have said, is a form of relationship), and a "yes" that is actually a "no" is one of the quickest ways to drain it.

There is a place for demands, instruction and telling people what to do. However, they are more prevalent in the domains of management, consulting and teaching rather than that of leading. In contrast, leadership requires choice and therefore, clear requests that can be accepted, denied or renegotiated are a more effective tool. However, in order to make such requests, the leader has to steer between making demands and living in expectations, both of which can be very tempting to the someone who is more concerned with protecting their image than with creating powerful relationships.

To review, the leadership fundamental of Purpose is therefore underpinned by the three Internal Pillars in the following ways:

- Mental State Pillar: knowing your purpose and that of the people around you.
- Emotional State Pillar: being emotionally attached to the importance of your purpose and the purpose of those around you.
- Physical State Pillar: taking action by making requests to enroll others into your purpose, and making offers to demonstrate that you are enrolled in the purpose of others.

From the first leadership fundamental of Purpose we move on to the second: Energy, your energy and the energy of those around you whom you hope to lead. As we shall see, these two leadership fundamentals are symbiotically linked.

24

ENERGY

Have you ever met anyone who said they wanted *less* energy? Neither have we. You can have a very solid idea of your purpose and the purpose of others in your Mental State Pillar, you might be emotionally connected to your purpose and the purpose of those around you in your Emotional State Pillar, but if you do not have the energy to make it happen in your Physical State Pillar, then it merely becomes interesting information and a nice feeling.

Energy is what allows you to translate the desired purpose into reality (which is the only place it really matters). Of course, energy on its own does not guarantee that you will achieve it, but without it, you are going nowhere.

Before we proceed, let's take a look at some science. According to the law of conservation of energy, the amount of energy within an isolated system remains constant, and is said to be conserved over time. This means that energy cannot be created or destroyed; within this system however, energy can be transformed (from one form to another) or transferred (from one object to another). We first saw this concept in Chapter 21: food contains energy; by eating and digesting food, we unlock the energy it contains for our own use.

THREE TYPES OF ENERGY AND PURPOSE

Human beings basically process three main types of energy, and these types of energy directly correlate to the three Internal Pillars of Performance:

- If I have the strength to achieve my goal, then I have the necessary physical energy towards the goal.
- If I am excited by my goal, then I have the necessary emotional energy towards the goal.
- If I think my goal is a good idea or the "right" thing to do, then I have the necessary mental energy towards the goal.

When I have a strong, emotionally-fuelled sense of purpose, then it creates focussed and aligned energy across the three Internal Pillars of Performance: the Physical, Mental and Emotional State Pillars.

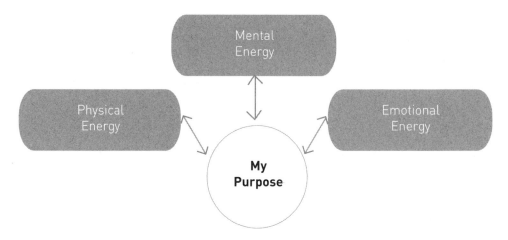

Figure 24.1 Fuelling Your Purpose with Three Types of Energy

Figure 24.1 illustrates the symbiotic relationship between Purpose and Energy. Find your purpose and the energies follow. Find your energies and your ability to achieve your purpose is strengthened.

In the domain of leadership, when your goal is to have people choose to follow you, it is important to remember that not everyone places the same value on each of these energies:

- Some people value action and busy-ness most highly. This is the energy of the Physical State Pillar and the ability to work hard.
- Other people value relationships most highly. This is the energy of the Emotional State Pillar and the ability to connect deeply with people and purpose.
- Others value intelligence most highly. This is the energy of the Mental State Pillar and the ability to figure things out.

Learning to build, maintain and use *your* energy is important, but in leadership, it is at least as important to be able to do the same for those around you. If you and your team are too tired to take action, build relationships and figure out the best plan of action, then the purpose is going to remain unrealised.

Which of these energies do you place the most value on? Which of these energies do the members of your team place the most value on?

OTHER PEOPLE'S ENERGY

Let's go back to the science for a moment. We know that energy within an isolated system can be transformed from form to form or transferred from object to object. Now, ask yourself the following questions. When you walk into the room, what happens to the energy of the people in that room? Do people leave your space energised or deflated? What impact do you have on people's energy?

If you have read the *Harry Potter* series, you will be familiar with the idea of a dementor, the ghastly creature that sucks the life force and energy out of all the people who encounter them.

"Dementors are among the foulest creatures that walk this earth. They infest the darkest, filthiest places, they glory in decay and despair, they drain peace, hope, and happiness out of the air around them... Get too near a Dementor and every good feeling, every happy memory will be sucked out of you."
- J. K. Rowling, *Harry Potter and the Prisoner of Azkaban*

I have met more than a few "office dementors". These people are usually completely unaware of the impact they have on others, and are shocked when someone shares their experience of being around them. Chances are that you know a dementor in your life, and if you don't, then it is probably *you* who is the dementor!

ENERGY IS A CHOICE

In your role as a leader, the ability to relate to someone so that they are energised is one of the key tasks before you. At first glance, you might think that someone's energy is their own affair and that you cannot do anything to influence it. Nothing could be further from the truth. One of the inconvenient little truths that people often do not want to face up to is that energy is a *choice*.

Increasingly, the people that we coach complain of being exhausted and burned out, and very often they have a great story (Singapore or Los Angeles? See Chapter 6) about why that is. Usually, it involves blaming their boss, their job, their kids or their spouse. Sometimes they blame themselves, which usually sounds like this: "I'm so exhausted because I'm bad at time management". In my experience, time management is never the cause; it is always the symptom. Rather, the cause is an unwillingness to say "no" or ask for support, as we have seen.

A lack of energy seems to be the curse of the 21st century. People repeat the "I'm tired" mantra over and over again until it becomes an acceptable and accepted justification for not doing something. What they are unwilling to face up to is that they are responsible for their own levels of energy.

Energy and the Mental State Pillar

This is, in our experience, less of an issue in corporate life. Most people spend an inordinate amount of time figuring out and arguing for the "right" strategy or the "right" thing to do. This is an important factor, but it is by no means the only important one, and so many leaders and bosses miss this. They figure that if they can convince other people that their strategy is the right strategy, then people will automatically be energised and follow them.

There's no doubt that for some people this is all that it takes, but when we coach people we are constantly struck by how their source of ennui often has nothing whatsoever to do with strategy and their Mental State Pillar. Instead, the factors that crop up time and time again are a lack of energy in the Emotional or Physical State Pillars.

Energy and the Physical State Pillar

People make nutritional choices (what to eat and when to eat), lifestyle choices (when to go to sleep and when to get up) and movement choices (whether to exercise and what type of exercise to do) all the time. These hour-to-hour choices have a fundamental impact on the level of physical energy that you possess. As we saw in Part II, your food and drink choices are crucial in this respect.

Nowadays, the desire for immediate comfort, coupled with an unwillingness to rest and relax, often leads to instant energy bursts driven by sugar and stimulants like caffeine. These choices in turn lead to energy crashes when the effects of the stimulant run out. People keep revving their internal engine, driving their body into their ground in a way that they would never think of doing with their cars. Learning how to manage your energy via your nutritional and resting choices is a key element to attaining peak performance.

As a leader, is it OK for you to talk to people about what they eat, when they eat and when they rest? That's up to you and how you see leadership. As we have said in Chapter 22, the involvement of the Physical State Pillar in leadership is only going to become more mainstream, but that does not mean you have to become a nutritionist in order to be a great leader. It is the whole ethos of this book that while you can give people the distinctions in a particular area and raise their awareness of the importance of these distinctions, you cannot force them to make any particular choice, however sensible it may seem to you. What you can do however is once the distinctions regarding energy and the Physical State Pillar are in place, you can work on the other forms of energy: the energy of the Emotional and Mental State Pillars. Once people feel emotionally connected to you and your purpose and mentally connected to your strategy and your ideas, then they are far more likely to manage their own physical energy, and even find reserves that they never realised that they had.

Walking the Talk

The other thing you can do, of course, is to set a good example when it comes to physical energy management. Are you paying attention to your nutritional choices? Are you taking small breaks throughout the day? Are you making full use of your annual leave? As with other areas of leadership, the people around you are far more likely to choose to follow you if you walk the talk. In a situation where you have hierarchical power, your behaviour sets the frame (consciously or otherwise) for the behaviour that is possible and acceptable for those around you.

Remember the distinction between being a "leader *for*" something versus being a "leader *of*" something in Chapter 23? This is a good place to make such a distinction. What are you leading *for* in this context? Are you creating an environment where people feel challenged and supported to manage their own physical energy in a responsible manner? Is this expected in your teams, or is "sleep for wimps" and "lunch for the lazy"? Consider the impact of your attitude in this fundamental area on the lives of the people around you.

Energy and the Emotional State Pillar

Depending on how connected they feel to their purpose, people can feel emotionally revved up or emotionally drained. We have looked at this before. As a leader, it is important for you to forge connections between your purpose and the purpose of those you wish to have follow you.

However, it is also critical that those people feel valued by you and believe that they are valuable to you. The need to feel valued and appreciated is fundamental to human beings. So often, especially in corporate life, leaders (or bosses) treat the people around them as pawns on a chessboard, as means to an end, and then wonder why those people show up as lacking in energy. One of the simplest and most overlooked ways to have people feel valued is to acknowledge them, to recognise them for their efforts. Of course, it has to be an authentic appreciation, not a fake or insincere acknowledgement.

Consider which people in your life you actually take the time to acknowledge. This can be very revealing. Pay attention to who is and who is not on your list. You may have some great stories about why you do not acknowledge someone ("Oh, they *know* I value them, they don't need me to tell them; that would be weird", etc.). However, at the end of the day, *everyone* appreciates being genuinely recognised and valued. If you notice that there is someone important missing from your list, then you can expect them be lacking in emotional energy when it comes to you and your leadership.

There are many ways that you can acknowledge people. It may be a matter of sitting down with someone and verbally telling them how much you appreciate their work, it may be celebrating victories together, sharing success or giving them flexibility over their time so that they can manage personal issues. Only by asking someone will you find out what they value most. Acknowledgement is far more effective when it coincides with what the other person sees as important, rather than simply being a reflection of what you see as important.

Barriers to Appreciation

There are very common beliefs that prevent people from showing their appreciation of others. Very often our clients say that they prefer not to show their appreciation because they are scared of the recipient relaxing or losing their edge as a result of being appreciated. Is that what happened to *you* when you received sincere acknowledgement? Did you relax and lose your edge or did you feel pumped up and energised?

In fact, in our experience we have found that this reason is usually a smokescreen. The real underlying barrier to giving acknowledgement is that, once again, it makes the giver vulnerable (we have already discussed this when it comes to making requests and offers in Chapter 23). If you sincerely appreciate someone, then it requires you to be open and to engage your emotions, and then they might think that you care or even perhaps want something else from them. Now you, or rather your image, is vulnerable to their assessment. But as we shall see in the next chapter, vulnerability can be a powerful way of connecting emotionally with the people around you.

If you can learn to develop your own energy levels, not just in the Mental State Pillar but also in the Physical and Emotional State Pillars, and help to build the energy levels of the people around you, then you will go long way to developing powerfully, both personally and as a leader.

25

RESILIENCE

In recent years, the leadership fundamental of Resilience, or "the ability to spring back into shape", has become a hot-button commodity in leadership development circles, and yet the vast majority of approaches proposed to develop it are very one-dimensional and limited. Most of these fall back into the trap of old-school training and development, tending to be overly focussed on the Mental State Pillar. In general, such approaches focus on developing the capacity to be resilient through intellectually learning about what it takes to be resilient, often through a study of how other people have done it in the past.

However, as we have seen many times in this book, *knowing* how to be resilient does not necessarily lead to someone *being* resilient (remember our burger-eating fellow who says he wants to lose weight and who knows how to do it, but decides *not* to act on it?). Intellectually-based resilience training tends to focus on mantras like "be positive," "focus on the bigger picture", "see every experience as a learning opportunity", "be gentle on yourself", "seek support", "find humour in the situation", and we could go on and on! Such mantras are all very well meaning, but giving people information on how to be resilient is not going to have them develop the ability to do it, especially under the stress of a very difficult situation.

In fact, knowing *how* to do it can actually make things worse! Once you know how to do it in your Mental State Pillar, the pressure is on you to translate that into action in your Physical State Pillar or to experience a different feeling in your Emotional State Pillar. If you believe that you know how to do it but don't do it, then you actually feel more stressed than you did before! Well-meaning knowledge transfer training can actually make things worse!

> *You can have as many theories as you want,*
> *but who you are willing to be in the world is what makes the difference.*

So, what is the alternative?

RESILIENCE AND THE PHYSICAL STATE PILLAR

If you are going to develop resilience, then the experience needs to begin in your body. You need to create the physical experience of being resilient, so that your whole system (Physical, Mental and Emotional State Pillars) knows that it can cope with and get through difficult experiences. In short, you need to develop the practice of *embodying* resilience, so that under pressure, when the circumstances really start closing in on you, you don't just have knowledge about what you *should* do, but you have direct physical experience of the fact that you *can* deal with this. It is nice to know what other people have done in the past to demonstrate resilience, but it is far more important to know that *you* have the capacity to be resilient.

Resilience, Comfort & Discomfort

However, you might now begin to see the problem. In Chapter 16, we looked at today's obsession with "comfort" and the corresponding allergic reaction to feeling any form of "discomfort". How can you practise embodying resilience or develop the capacity to be resilient if you are unwilling to be uncomfortable in the first place? In short, you can't. These factors are linked.

Resilience has become a hot-button issue in leadership development today precisely because people nowadays are obsessed with experiencing comfort and avoiding discomfort. In years gone by, people experienced more discomfort more often in their life, and therefore, they developed a direct experience of developing resilience in reality, not in a training room. Nowadays however, the strong desire to experience comfort has stripped people of the real-time, physical state learning regarding resilience. You do not need resilience in the face of comfort; you need it in the face of discomfort. So, as people become more comfortable, the need for resilience disappears, and consequently, so does the opportunity to develop it through day-to-day living. Fast forward a decade and *boom*, suddenly there is a resilience deficit in leadership. What a shocker.

In true 21st-century fashion, the response is to try and develop resilience in the most comfortable way possible: sitting in a training room, reading books and looking at Powerpoint slides, learning about resilience and listening to inspiring stories about how other people have exhibited it in the past.

Resilience and Discomfort

An alternative approach is to repeatedly put yourself in experiences where you feel discomfort of some kind and yet come out on the other side. This is how you develop resilience: through physical practice. There are many possible practices you could choose to develop an experience of "discomfort", but as we saw in Part II, regular exercise can be a great way to do it because it can generate discomfort in your physical, mental and emotional states all in one go!

Remember however that there is no inherent link between the practice and the capacity you are looking to develop; instead you need to decide and be conscious about why you are doing what you are doing. As we saw previously, not all forms of exercise are equally useful in this respect. If you want to experience discomfort and then experience overcoming it, then a form of exercise where your Physical, Mental and Emotional State Pillars are simultaneously challenged to their limits before recovering is likely to be more effective than exercise where the challenge is less intense.

For example, 30-minute HIIT sessions will work more effectively than easy jogging on a treadmill for the same amount of time. Anyone who has regularly done HIIT sessions will know what I mean. It is specifically designed for you to practise discomfort in all states and then practise coming back to some sort of equilibrium. By doing HIIT sessions, you not only boost your health, you also embody resilience and develop the capacity for the "bounce-back-ability" that seems to be so lacking in 21st-century leaders.

So, in order to develop resilience, you cannot simply rely on developing your Mental State Pillar. The willingness to include your Physical State Pillar makes a big impact. Similarly, engaging your Emotional State Pillar in your drive to develop a capacity for resilience is also highly beneficial.

RESILIENCE AND THE EMOTIONAL STATE PILLAR

This aspect is linked to our first leadership fundamental: Purpose. If you want to develop resilience, then it is important to be clear on your purpose and make sure that the purpose is one to which you are *emotionally* connected. When you are emotionally connected to and invested in something, you will notice that resilience comes a whole lot easier.

Think about it: if you have kids, do you need to build your capacity to keep on loving them? No, you don't, because you care about them. You are emotionally connected to your kids and so (most of the time!) it does not even feel like you *need* resilience to deal with any discomfort you might feel along the way. Instead, it just becomes what you do.

PERSONAL REFLECTION

Marcus: Resilience and the Emotional State Pillar

When my mother was diagnosed with cancer and subsequently passed away, it was an incredibly difficult time for me as I was living halfway around the world at the time. The grieving process over the last nine months of her life was incredibly intense and punctuated with many days when the last thing I wanted to do was to coach other people on *their* life. After all, I was in such turmoil about my own life.

However, as I look back on it now, it was a good example of an emotional connection to a purpose keeping someone on track. I love my work. It does not feel like a job to me, rather it feels like something that I am called to do—a vocation, if you will. It was that emotional connection to what I was doing at the time of my mother's passing that really kept me going, despite wanting at times to just throw everything in a suitcase, jump on a plane, and be by her side. I know it would have been a lot tougher for me to keep going and "bounce back" from watching her suffer if I had been in a job which I felt little or no emotional connection towards.

In short, you don't need resilience quite so much if you are passionate about what you are working on.

Emotional Connection, Cynicism and Vulnerability

In recent years, resilience has disappeared, not only because have people stopped experiencing the practice ground of discomfort, but also because "passion" and "emotional connection" to a sense of purpose have gone out of fashion, especially in today's workplace. It is far more fashionable to be cynical than passionate. Cynicism is passed off for wisdom and passion is passed off as naïvety: "Oh, you actually *care* about this company? That's so cute. I used to care too, but I learned, and soon enough so will you." Maybe someone has said that to you, or maybe you have actually said it to someone else! Sometimes, of course, this is not expressed verbally, but it is very clear that it is the implied message.

To emotionally connect with someone or something is to experience the emotional state of vulnerability, and today, the experience of "vulnerability" is even less attractive than the experience of "discomfort". The word "vulnerability" comes from *vulnera*, the Latin word which means "to wound". When you allow yourself to be emotionally connected to something or someone, or in this case, your purpose, you become vulnerable because you expose what matters to you. When you do this there is the possibility of being ridiculed for your passion, or even of someone taking away that to which you are so intimately connected. There is no free lunch: emotional connection brings passion, energy and excitement, but it also makes you vulnerable to attack.

The aspect of the Mental State Pillar that facilitates vulnerability is this belief or assessment: "I am enough". If you truly believe this about yourself, then you create the possibility of opening up and being vulnerable, because you have nothing to fear by opening up and letting people in. For as long as you believe you are "not enough", "bad" or lacking in some way, you will resist being open and vulnerable because you fear that when people really see you, they will see what you see in yourself—that you are not enough.

PERSONAL REFLECTION

Marcus: Vulnerability

As with many of the factors I have discussed in this book, vulnerability only really matters when it shows up in action, rather than as a concept in your mind. Although vulnerability is an experience which shows up in the Emotional State Pillar, it only makes a difference when it shows up in your Physical State Pillar: when you take action in a vulnerable manner. Sari has taught me about the power of vulnerability over the last 10 years, without saying a word or using a single Powerpoint slide. It is one of the qualities that I respect and love about her the most.

When I first met Sari, she was a young lady from Central Java living in Jakarta. She had already made one big move in her life by leaving the safe environs of her small hometown and jumping into big city life. When we met, things began to move quickly and new experiences began to arrive for her thick and fast, including changing careers and competing in fitness competitions in Singapore, then in Southeast Asia, and then on a world stage in Europe. She won in Singapore and Southeast Asia, but did not place in Europe. It did not stop her. She decided to certify as a professional coach with NFA and then with the International Coach Federation, and now she is delivering leadership workshops and women's presence trainings.

Sari never stops "putting herself out there" and at each stage she makes herself vulnerable to failure, criticism and judgement. It does not stop her from moving forward and taking new ground. It is a quality that I find truly inspirational and also one that brings up a challenge for me: on the one hand, as her husband, I feel a desire to protect her and keep her safe, but on the other hand, I know that this is one of the qualities that makes her so special and ultimately what makes her who she is in the world.

This quality of vulnerability is one that I am constantly working to develop in myself. The willingness to be vulnerable has never been a capacity that I have found easy to build, but living with my wife as a role model in this regard has certainly inspired me to keep practising it and moving forward in my own life. It is a quality that is critical in leadership, because when you open yourself up to be vulnerable you create the possibility of letting someone else into your life, and by so doing you are able to develop a far deeper relationship than is possible if you were to remain safe and closed.

Writing a book is an act of vulnerability in itself and in many ways, this book is only finally being written because of Sari's constant willingness to be vulnerable over many years and her encouragement to me to do the same. Sari has been a leader *for* vulnerability, not in words but in action, and I have chosen to follow her on that path.

Sometimes, of course, you can be so emotionally connected to something (or someone) that when you lose it (or think you are in danger of losing it) that you feel unsteady and require resilience to get through it. Emotional connection to a purpose is not a panacea that will forever remove the need for resilience, but it can significantly reduce the occasions where resilience is required. Whenever I am emotionally connected to my purpose I will automatically find reserves of resilience, ones that I will never find if I am working on something in which I am not emotionally invested.

Along the way, your ability to bounce back may be compromised by two key sets of assessments:

1. "I cannot do this. I cannot keep going."

   The most powerful way to combat this assessment is to provide evidence to yourself that you *can* keep going. This is where the Physical State Pillar helps you. If you are willing to practise experiencing and recovering from discomfort, then you can begin to embody the experience of resilience. This proves to your Mental State Pillar that you *can* keep going, because you have done so in the past.

2. "This is not important. I don't want to keep going."

   The most powerful way to combat this assessment is to become very clear on *why* you are doing what you are doing. This is where the Emotional

State Pillar helps you. If you are willing to practise experiencing emotional connection and the vulnerability that comes with it, then you can learn to resist the urge to give up.

The emergence of resilience as a major trend in leadership development is very revealing of 21st-century life: the resilience deficit is showing up today because of an unwillingness to experience discomfort and vulnerability. A one-dimensional mental approach towards resilience training is never going to overcome that. However, by involving the Emotional and Physical State Pillars of Performance and linking them to the Mental State Pillar, you can build a capacity for resilience far more effectively.

26

MOVEMENT

The final fundamental of leadership is Movement. In many respects, everything so far in the book has been leading up to this point: the importance of movement in leadership. It has been the lack of mention of body and movement in leadership discourses for many years that led to us creating SPI, developing the Five Pillars of Performance, and ultimately writing this book.

Movement is fundamental to leadership, because essentially, it is what leaders do: they move themselves and others towards a new goal. If a leader cannot move other people, then they are not really a leader. Remember our discussion on leadership in Chapter 22? Leadership involves having other people choose to follow you. This process takes place in *action*, in *reality*, not in some abstract theory. No movement means no leadership. It is as simple as that.

The problem is, so many people in business today are so busy focussing on their career or profession that they don't create space to practise movement. Little do they know that this lack of a capacity for effective movement is ultimately a major factor that ends up holding them back in their career!

Movement is similar to resilience in this respect: you can *learn* about it or you can build a capacity to *embody* it effectively and efficiently. As with resilience, if you want to develop the capacity to move effectively and efficiently, then you need to develop a practice that requires you to physically move.

BORN TO MOVE

In Part II, we saw that in order to learn, know, develop and grow, ultimately you need to be willing to involve your body. However, your body actually needs to *move*! Movement is fundamental to our whole system; as a species we have evolved to move. When we stop moving, we stop learning and knowing. Movement is inherently linked to life itself. When your lungs stop moving and your blood stops flowing, you have a problem!

The cerebellum is the part of the brain specifically charged with "motor function" or movement. This has been well known for some time, but what is becoming increasingly clear is that the cerebellum also plays a significant role in cognition and learning. Until recently, it was held to be true that the neocortex dealt with thinking, whilst the cerebellum dealt with movement; this thinking was really a by-product of the belief in the separation of mind and body. Increasingly, this dualistic approach is being superseded and the role of the cerebellum in cognitive function and even in emotions is being recognised. This still-developing understanding of the integrated role of the cerebellum lends more weight to the thinking outlined in this book: that the Physical, Mental and Emotional State Pillars are not only all critical in effective action and leadership, but they are also all inseparably linked and integrated in their utility.

MOVEMENT AND LEADERSHIP

For human beings, as we have repeatedly seen, the pull of repetition and comfort is very strong. Once we become good at a game, we like to form habits to repeat our success. However, if you want to continue to learn, grow, develop and truly lead, then the importance of continuing to move cannot be overestimated.

The importance of movement can be seen in our everyday language: I say "I am stuck" when I cannot move physically, mentally or emotionally. Movement is not simply a phenomenon of the Physical State Pillar, it has equally powerful components that show up in the Mental and Emotional State Pillars.

Of course, the phrase "to move" is also linked to the Emotional State Pillar, not only the Physical State Pillar. As we have seen in this book, it is our emotions that move us most powerfully in life, not our thoughts. I may *think* something is a good idea, but it is only when I am *emotionally connected* to that idea that I will actually create sustained activity (or movement) towards getting it done.

Movement is also strongly linked to the Mental State Pillar. Are you willing to move your thinking? Remember the "X's" and "O's" and the importance of "being open" from the Overview of this book? The willingness to be open in your approach to life is ultimately a willingness to move your thinking.

Similarly, in leadership, are you able to engage with people such that they experience movement in *their* Emotional and Mental State Pillars? If all they do is feel different or simply follow you blindly without shifting their point of view, then your leadership is unlikely be consistently effective. In both of these domains, as in the Physical State Pillar, a lack of movement leads to a state of disrepair. This diminishes your capacity for personal and leadership development, which is all about connection and your willingness to engage and relate.

BARRIERS TO MOVEMENT

Given the importance of movement, why is it that people don't move? Perhaps they see no value in moving, because it is more comfortable to stay where they are. In that case, you need to understand and connect whatever *you* are leading for to *their* purpose and why they are emotionally connected to it. Even if their Mental State Pillar *understands* the value in moving, they might not have the energy from the Emotional and Physical State Pillars to move. As we have already seen, purpose is fuelled by energy from the Physical, Mental and Emotional State Pillars:

- If you are burning people out, they will lack energy from the Physical State Pillar.
- If they are not feeling valued by you, they will lack energy from the Emotional State Pillar.
- If you have not convinced them that this is the best course of action, they will lack energy from the Mental State Pillar.

Even if they see value in moving and have the necessary energy, they may simply have stopped because the going got too tough. If that is the case, do they lack resilience? If they lack resilience, then what have you done to build that capacity in them? Have you been stretching them so that they have experienced the cycle of discomfort and recovery, or have you been controlling, micromanaging and protecting them from discomfort? Have you been (re-)connecting them to their purpose so that they keep on keeping on, or have you merely been forcing *your* purpose down their throats, so that their emotional connection to the goal remains weak?

SARIUS DYNAMIC ENERGETICS: GETTING READY

In Part II we looked at the seven basic functional movements that are important to consciously and correctly practise if you want to move effectively as a human being. Now, in Part III, we will make some finer distinctions in movement to link them to leadership itself. Conscious movement in your Physical State Pillar can help you develop capacities in your Mental and Emotional State Pillars.

These five capacities, which we have termed "Dynamic Energetics", consist of:

- Stability
- Flexibility
- Strength
- Power
- Restoration

These are important factors in both personal effectiveness and leadership. We have called them "Dynamic Energetics", because they involve ways of shifting your energy such that you can create specific valuable experiences in the world, for yourself and for others.

Alignment, Breathing and the Core

Before we dive into the Dynamic Energetics proper, let's start with the basics: Alignment, Breathing and the Core (or "ABC" for short). It is important to incorporate these elements into all of your movement practices if you are to reap maximum benefit from the Dynamic Energetics.

Alignment

The practice of alignment is designed to maintain optimum postural integrity whenever you move. Aligned posture involves stacking your body's segments from head to shoulders, to hips, knees and feet, in a proper manner to allow your body to function best as a whole.

To practise alignment, stand with your feet parallel and shoulder-width apart, belly tucked in, shoulders pulled back and moving away from your ears, with chest lifted and head neutral. From the side, the centre of your ear, shoulder, hip, knee, and ankle should form a straight line. Avoid a forward head, rounded shoulders, protruding belly, excessive curve in the lower back and hyperextended knees. Tip: stand tall and be proud.

Breathing

Usually unconscious and automatic, breathing influences and is influenced by our Physical, Mental and Emotional State Pillars. Becoming conscious of your breathing and adapting your habitual patterns is one of the simplest and yet most profound shifts that you can make. In our experience, performance can be significantly improved by suitable respiratory training and adopting a practice of breathing that involves your diaphragm. This is especially true when performing at high intensity. Conscious breathing plays a big part in maintaining postural integrity and performance.

To practise conscious breathing, put your hands on and around your rib cage. When you breathe in through your nose, the rib cage should expand laterally. When you breathe out through your mouth (think of blowing through a straw), slightly draw your belly in toward your lower back. When moving your body, inhale on the easier motion and exhale on the harder motion. Bring this thought to your mind as you breathe:

Breathing facilitates movement. When you breathe well, you move well.

Tip: when in doubt, breathe out. Don't hold your breath for too long!

Core

Your core is a complex series of muscles in the centre of your body. It involves all the muscles in that area. Think of your core as a cylinder with the diaphragm as a lid on top, the pelvis floor at the base, and the muscles that surround it like a corset. Your core is an important element in everything that you do: standing up, moving yourself and moving other things.

To engage your core, start in the standing position. Place one hand on your stomach, an inch below your belly button, and your other hand on the side of your ribcage. Breathe in through your nose and feel your ribcage expand. Breathe out through your mouth, drawing the region just below your navel towards your spine and maintaining an upright posture. Imagining your corset has a frontal zip, gently zip it from bottom to top and keep it tight while breathing in and out.

You should feel a gentle tightening under the hand on your stomach when you engage your core correctly. Tip: think of your core as a solid tree trunk in the middle of a storm.

Practice

Remember to apply the ABCs when you practise the Dynamic Energetics. Here is a brief summary of the three elements of ABC:

- Alignment: stand tall and be proud.
- Breathing: inhale and exhale consciously.
- Core: keep it tight!

As you practise your ABCs, pay attention to what happens in your Physical, Mental and Emotional State Pillars. Ask yourself these questions:

- What values do I want to embody as I move through the space?
- Where do I notice these values in my body (if they exist at all)?

Aligned and ready to move? Here we go!

27

SARIUS DYNAMIC ENERGETICS

IMPORTANT

Before you begin any of the Dynamic Energetic movements outlined in this chapter, please note the following. Fill up the Physical Activity Readiness Questionnaire (PAR-Q) provided in Appendix II before you proceed. All forms of exercise pose some inherent risks. We advise our readers to know their limits and take full responsibility for your own safety. Do not take risks beyond your level of experience, training and fitness. If you experience pain while doing these movements, stop immediately and consult your physician.

STABILITY

We define stability as the capacity to stay on purpose in the presence of change. In the Physical State Pillar, stability creates body control in the presence of change and builds the ability to resist an undesired movement. It is a quality or state of something that is not easily moved from its purpose.

Developing a stability practice in the Physical State Pillar builds the capacity to stay on purpose in the Mental State Pillar and the capacity to create an experience of certainty and consistency in the Emotional State Pillar.

The purpose of stability practice is to increase your body control by engaging your core throughout all four movements. To start, we recommend five repetitions for each movement. You can increase the number of reps as you progress.

FLEXIBILITY

We define flexibility as the capacity to flow or move with ease in the presence of tensity. In the Physical State Pillar, flexibility is the normal extensibility of all tissues that allow full range of motion of a joint. However, for soft tissue to achieve efficient extensibility there must be optimum control throughout the entire range of motion. More specifically, this optimum control can be referred to as dynamic range of motion. This is the combination of flexibility and the nervous system's ability to control this range of motion efficiency (or neuromuscular efficiency).[14]

Developing a flexibility practice in the Physical State Pillar builds the capacity to move with ease and flow and be creative in the Mental State Pillar and the capacity to create an experience of lightness in the Emotional State Pillar.

The purpose of flexibility practice is to increase your range of motion and move well. As with your stability practice, there are four movements. Start off with five reps for each movement and increase the number of reps as you progress.

---

14   NASM. *NASM Essentials of Personal Fitness Training.*

STRENGTH

We define strength as the capacity to persevere in the presence of resistance. In the Physical State Pillar, strength is the ability of the neuromuscular system to produce internal tension to overcome an external force.[15] It is the ability to carry out work in the face of resistance.

Developing a strength practice in the Physical State Pillar builds the capacity to persevere in the Mental State Pillar and the capacity to create an experience of tenacity in the Emotional State Pillar.

The purpose of strength practice is to build your strength by overcoming external force. In these movements, you will work with a partner, who represents an external force outside your own body. Ideally, pick a partner with the same height as you, but adapt if your partner is taller or shorter! If you have no partner, don't worry; the sample training plan in Appendix III provides a list of exercises for individual practice.

There are four movements here, and they are most effectively carried out in a circuit (doing each movement consecutively without rest), with a one-minute break in between each circuit. Begin with two circuits of 10 reps per movement and increase the number of reps or circuits as your body adapts to the challenge.

Here are some tips when working with your partner:

- Your goal is to maintain the tension the entire time you are moving with your partner.
- The resistance that you apply to your partner should not be intense or jerky. You want to make each other really work for every movement. However, you do not want to resist so hard that the other person cannot move.
- Aim for tempo-controlled movement together.

---

15   NASM. *NASM Essentials of Personal Fitness Training.*

POWER

We define power as the capacity to generate impact in the presence of a challenge. In the Physical State Pillar, power is defined as the ability of muscles to exert maximal force output in a minimal amount of time (also known as "rate of production").[16] It plays an important role in athletic performance and general fitness improvements. Power also requires the element of speed. A strong upper body may be able to lift big weights but lack the ability to throw a javelin very far if enough speed cannot be generated. Simply put, when you have strength *and* speed, you have power.

Developing a power practice in the Physical State Pillar builds the capacity to make an impact in the Mental State Pillar and the capacity to create an experience of excitement in the Emotional State Pillar.

The purpose of power practice is to train your brain and muscles to work together faster and more effectively, thereby creating a high-impact movement. The most effective way to develop power is through two forms of training: plyometrics and SAQ (speed, agility and quickness) training. Plyometrics, also known as jump training, involve exercises that generate quick, powerful movements involving an explosive concentric contraction, followed immediately by an explosive concentric contraction.[17] SAQ training combines three related but different abilities: speed, agility and quickness. Speed is defined as the ability to move the body in one intended direction as fast as possible. Agility refers to the ability to start, stop, and change direction quickly, while maintaining proper posture. Quickness is the ability to react and change body position with a maximum rate of force production, in all planes of motion, from all body positions, during functional activities.[18]

These exercises are more advanced than the movements that have come before, and are best incorporated after you have achieved core stability, strength, proper range of motion and an overall strength base.

There are three plyometric movements. Within one minute, complete five repetitions of each movement. Focus on the quality of your movements first,

---

16   NASM. *NASM Essentials of Personal Fitness Training.*

17   NASM. *NASM Essentials of Personal Fitness Training.*

18   NASM. *NASM Essentials of Personal Fitness Training.*

then work your way up to eight repetitions of each movement in one minute as you progress. There is only one SAQ exercise (the Cone Drill), but it incorporates the sprint, back pedal and side shuffle to make one explosive exercise! This drill is designed to be performed in short bursts at maximum speed.

RESTORATION

Finally we come to restoration, which we define as the capacity to recover in the presence of completion. In the Physical State Pillar, restoration is a process of recovery, a movement or return to a particular state, in preparation for the next movement. Most easily defined as a combination of sleep and time spent not training, restoration is the simplest Dynamic Energetic to understand and implement. It is also therefore often the easiest to overlook.

Developing a restoration practice in the Physical State Pillar builds the capacity to recover in the Mental State Pillar and the capacity to create an experience of calmness in the Emotional State Pillar.

The purpose of restoration practice is to slow down and establish a sense of peace. As with the other Dynamic Energetics, there are four movements: for each stretching movement we recommend holding the stretch for five slow breathes as a way to get started.

Now, let's get to the Sarius Dynamic Energetics! As you work through these movements, always keep your ABCs in mind: keep yourself aligned, breathe fully and consciously, and keep your core braced.

STABILITY PRACTICE

1 HIP RAISE

Lie on your back, knees bent and feet flat on the floor, shoulder-width apart, hands by your side. Pressing your arms to the floor, squeeze your buttocks and raise your hips off the floor. Your body should form a straight line from your shoulders to your knees. Pause at the top for two seconds, then slowly return to starting position.

Imagine a pillow between your inner thighs; squeeze it gently while keeping your knees pointing forwards.

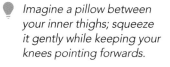

2 OPPOSITE ARM AND LEG EXTENSION

Kneel on all fours, aligning your shoulders over your wrists and your hips over your knees. Lift and straighten one leg to hip height, then reach forward with the opposite hand. Hold for two seconds, then return to starting position.

Imagine a bowl of water on top of your tailbone. Keep the bowl steady throughout this exercise.

STABILITY PRACTICE

3 TORSO TWIST

Sit cross-legged and form a circle with your arms, fingertips touching. Keeping your hips facing forward, slowly rotate your upper body 45 degrees to the right. Return to the centre and repeat on your left side.

💡 *Throughout this exercise, keep your hands directly in front of your chest; they should follow your upper body as it rotates. For modification, you can do this exercise sitting on a chair.*

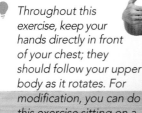

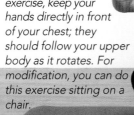

4 OVERHEAD SQUAT

Stand with feet shoulder-width apart and knees pointed straight ahead. Raise your arms overhead with straight elbows, palms facing each other. Push your hips back as if you are about to sit on a chair and lower your body until your thighs are parallel to the floor. Hold for two counts at the bottom, then return to starting position.

💡 *As you squat, keep your kneecaps in line with your middle toes. Do not let them move excessively forward such that your heels come off the ground, which places unnecessary stress on the knees. This is a challenging exercise. To make it easier, you can do it with your arms extended in front of your chest.*

FLEXIBILITY PRACTICE

1 SPINAL CURVE

Kneel on all fours, aligning your shoulders over your wrists and your hips over your knees. Breathe in and slowly arch your back, dropping belly towards the floor, raising your head, chest and tailbone up. Hold for two counts. Breathe out and slowly round your back, pulling your belly inwards, dropping your head and tailbone down. Hold for two counts.

💡 *Don't overuse your lower back muscles. Let gravity do most of the work!*

2 SPINAL TWIST WITH ARM RAISE

Stand with your feet shoulder-width apart, raising your arms both sides. Keeping your shoulders down and legs in a fixed position, turn your chest towards your left. Hold for two seconds, then return to starting position before switching to the other side. Do five repetitions on each side.

💡 *Stretch your arms as far as you can, as if they are being pulled in opposite directions.*

3 MULTI-DIRECTIONAL ARM REACH

Stand upright, feet shoulder-width apart, arms by your sides, palms turned in. Step forward, reaching your arms forward at the same time. Then slowly raise your arms and reach towards the ceiling.

Step and shift your weight to the side, reaching up high and sideways. Hold for two counts in each position and then slowly return to the centre. Do five repetitions on each side.

Imagine making an offering when you reach forward. Keep an open body position and aim high as you reach up. Smile when you reach sideways.

FLEXIBILITY PRACTICE

4 MULTI-DIRECTIONAL LUNGE

Stand with feet shoulder-width apart, hands on your hips. Step forward, lowering your hips slowly until both knees are bent at about a 90-degree angle. Align your front knee over your ankle and maintain upper body straight while your other knee almost touches the floor. Keep the weight in your heels as you push back up to the starting position.

Progress to side lunges, followed by turning lunges.

💡 *Imagine a dancer walking or turning with lightness and confidence in their steps.*

STRENGTH PRACTICE

1 PARTNER PUSH

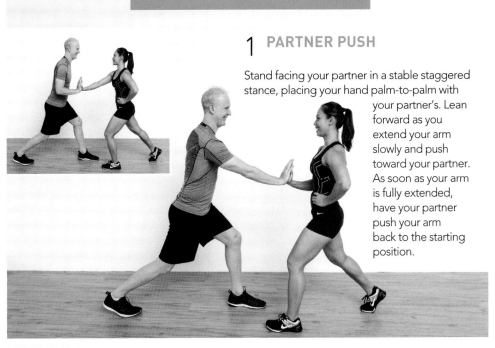

Stand facing your partner in a stable staggered stance, placing your hand palm-to-palm with your partner's. Lean forward as you extend your arm slowly and push toward your partner. As soon as your arm is fully extended, have your partner push your arm back to the starting position.

2 PARTNER PULL

Begin as in the Partner Push, but this time, clasp your partner's hand. Pull your partner toward you, driving your elbow to the back while your partner resists the pull, slowly extending their arm. As soon as your partner's arm is fully extended, your partner should start pulling back while you resist.

STRENGTH PRACTICE

3 PARTNER LUNGE

Stand facing each other about one foot apart in the lunge position. In this move, one of you will lunge forward while the other lunges backward. When you lunge forward with your right foot, your partner should respond by lunging backward with their left foot. When your partner lunges forward with their left foot, lunge backward with your right foot.

4 PARTNER WEIGHTED BALL TWIST

Stand back-to-back with a partner, feet hip-width apart, in a ready position. Hold the weighted ball by keeping elbows bent and the ball close to your body. Twist toward each other, pass the ball to your partner. Twist to the opposite side and receive the ball from your partner.

POWER PRACTICE

1 SQUAT JUMP

Stand with feet shoulder-width apart, knees pointing straight ahead. Jump up powerfully, extending arms overhead. Land as quietly as possible, returning your arms to the sides and your body into the squat position. Hold for two seconds, reset your posture before you jump again.

💡 *When you jump, do it powerfully like Bruce Lee. When you land, do it quietly like a ninja.*

2 ROTATIONAL WEIGHTED BALL SLAM

Stand with feet wider than shoulder-width apart. Pick the ball up on one side of your body, raise it overhead and rotate to the other side, pivoting your back foot. As you pivot, slam the ball down, bend your knees and sink down as you slam. Then, staying low, pick the ball back up, repeating the movement on the other side.

💡 *Draw a rainbow using the medicine ball and slam it to the ground in a swift and powerful motion!*

POWER PRACTICE

3 LATERAL BOUND

Stand on one foot, positioning your body
into a half squat. Hop from one side to the
other, maintaining optimum alignment.
Upon landing, immediately push off in the
opposite direction, returning to your original
start position. Repeat as quickly as you can
control the movement.

 Channel your inner ice-skater!

POWER PRACTICE

4 CONE DRILL

This timed drill is done facing the same direction the whole time. Set up five cones as shown below; cones A, B, D and E should be about two to three metres apart from cone C. Starting at cone A, move quickly from cone to cone, touching each cone you pass. Go for three attempts and get your best timing! Here's the full sequence:

1. A-B : sprint
2. B-C : back pedal
3. C-D : side shuffle
4. D-E : side shuffle
5. E-C : side shuffle
6. C-A : back pedal

💡 *Bring out the world-class footballer in you!*

Sprint

Back pedal

Side shuffle

RESTORATION PRACTICE

1 FRONT STRETCH

Stand in a standing lunge pose, hips facing front, front knee bent and hands by your side. Raise your arms over your head with your palms facing each other. Keep your shoulders relaxed and chest lifted. Switch to the other side.

💡 *Think of your body as a train track running from your toes to your fingertips. Try to lengthen the distance between one station and the other.*

2 BACK STRETCH

Stand with feet shoulder-width apart. From the starting position, reach forward with your arms at shoulder height. Bend forward at the hips with your upper body parallel to the floor, your head between your arms.

💡 *To modify, rest your hands on a chair or on a wall. Feel the stretch on your hamstrings and back. Relax and stretch more deeply as you exhale.*

RESTORATION PRACTICE

3   SIDE STRETCH

Stand with your feet wider than shoulder-width apart, resting one hand on a yoga block in front of your leg. Keeping your head centred, lift up from the waist and bend to one side, extending your free arm above your ear. Feel the stretch all the way down to your hips. Hold for five breaths, then return to the centre and switch sides.

Keep your feet firmly on the floor and when you feel tension, breathe into it.

4   TWIST STRETCH

Lie on your back. Bend one knee and cross it over the opposite leg. Gently pull your knee across your body as you twist your torso in the opposite direction. Extend the other hand and turn your face towards it. Keep both shoulders squared and rooted to the floor. Stay here for five deep breaths, then repeat on the other side.

Feel the stretch mostly on your lower back. Use a yoga strap to assist and deepen the pose, if required.

HOW DID YOU FEEL?

Once you have completed the Sarius Dynamic Energetics workout, we want you to pay close attention to how you felt while you were doing the movements. Rank the Dynamic Energetics in order of your level of comfort for each set of movements, starting from most comfortable (or easiest) to least comfortable (or most difficult).

1.

2.

3.

4.

5.

BENEFITS

Now, let's examine each set of movements and how they can benefit your everyday performance, both personally and as a leader.

Stability

For the "everyday athlete", core stability is an excellent way to promote the mobility and strength of your entire body in a variety of essential positions and movements throughout your whole body. The overhead squat is one of the most challenging yet effective practices we use when working with a client in the area of leadership presence, as it promotes stability in the face of high-pressure situations.

Core stability influences the way you stand and walk, as well as the tonality of your voice. Simply put, if you are capable of developing a stable core, it can allow you to engage others on a different level. As with all conscious movement, practising core stability with proper form requires constant attention.

Flexibility

In the flexibility domain, we build up movement from the ground to a standing position, working in multiple directions of movement. Beginning with an easy movement, we progress to more and more complex movements; the intention is for you to become aware of your space and how you move within space. A leader is required to move in multiple directions, not just one.

We all have our own personal space as well as the space that we share with others. Sometimes, the boundary between the two may not be clear for you or the people around you. Too much flexibility results in a loose boundary and confusion. Too much rigidity results in an environment where it is "hard to breathe". In the presence of tensity, what we need is a capacity for lightness and to move purposefully.

In combination with stability, flexibility training prepares the body to move well and with greater intensity. An uplifted posture and core stability can result in an altered perspective. Being firm with your own boundaries can keep you straight when needed, while at the same time, expanding your range of motion will allow you to see more possibilities.

Strength

We have incorporated a partner workout for this Dynamic Energetic because leadership involves other people. These movements will allow you to explore how you relate to another human being. The focus of strength movements is to perform with excellence in the face of resistance and pressure from forces external to your own body.

The emphasis of the strength practice is not on getting bigger muscles, but rather on building the capacity to keep going and adapt to new demands or external forces. You are working to build your internal toughness in overcoming stress, rather than seeking to avoid stress altogether. Simply put, in the strength practice you are working to have a healthy relationship with resistance.

Pay attention to your capacity to keep going forward in the face of resistance. Conversely, also notice your beliefs regarding giving resistance or pressure to others.

Power

Our approach in the power practice is not "the more the merrier" or "the longer the better"; instead we are looking at how to create impactful movement in a limited time as well as how to turn challenge into excitement. It teaches us how to use the whole body as one unit quickly and aggressively. This practice is designed to improve balance, power and neuromuscular firing patterns.

The Cone Drill is one particularly powerful form of SAQ training. It consists of short, intense drills that involve quick acceleration and deceleration while moving backward, forward or sideways. As leaders, we are required to move and reach out in many directions. It is important to build the capacity and embody the ability to be alert, agile and precise, all in a short time. SAQ training is about bringing all these elements together and learning how to work with momentum. It certainly brings the heart rate up too!

Restoration

There are times to push your limits and experience discomfort, but there are also times to acknowledge your limits and return to your comfort zone. In the flexibility practice, you work to expand your range of motion; here in the restoration practice, you are practising "surrendering" and acceptance.

For some people, lying relaxed on the ground is the most difficult posture of all! You may think you have completely relaxed and released all the tension, but in fact you may notice you are still holding on to some tension somewhere, somehow. The key here is to not force your body into a certain pose, but just to relax and breathe.

TRE® (see Chapter 14) is highly recommended to supplement your restoration program.

28

BUILDING CAPACITIES AND EXPERIENCES

Taken together, the Sarius Dynamic Energetic movements form an integrated set of capacities that are vital if you wish to develop your effectiveness and your leadership in particular. Once you know your purpose (Mental State Pillar) and you are emotionally connected to it (Emotional State Pillar), you can use movement in your Physical State Pillar to develop the following capacities in yourself and in others. Figure 28.1 shows each Dynamic Energetic with its corresponding capacity and experience:

Dynamic Energetic	Capacity	Experience
Stability	To stay on purpose	Certainty
Flexibility	To move with flow	Lightness
Strength	To persevere	Tenacity
Power	To generate impact	Excitement
Restoration	To recover	Calmness

Figure 28.1 Dynamic Energetics, Capacities & Experiences

These capacities are crucial to your success as a leader. You will not be able to manifest your purpose if you lack the capacity to stay on track (Stability), or if you lack the capacity to keep going (Strength) and get around the inevitable obstacles that will appear in your way (Flexibility). Equally, if you lack the capacity to create impact in the world (Power), no one will notice your efforts. Finally, if you are spent after one go-around and lack the capacity to recover (Restoration), then you are unlikely to go the distance and achieve your purpose.

In our experience working with clients, we have found a marked correlation between their ability to perform the movements of a specific Dynamic Energetic and their ability to exhibit the corresponding capacity. For instance, people who find it easy to stay on purpose and be stable are also comfortable with the movements associated with the Dynamic Energetic of Stability. This is not an accident; the movements are physical manifestations of the capacity. Similarly, people who have a well-developed capacity for perseverance and are described as tenacious are generally more comfortable with the Strength movements.

Of course, these capacities are not *inherent* in the movements; you have to be aware of the potential link and consciously focus on it as you perform the movements. Conscious movement is what makes the difference.

BUILDING CAPACITIES WITH CARDIOVASCULAR EXERCISE

Another element to consider is the type of cardio work that you do. Take two of the most common types of cardio machines: the treadmill and the static machine (the cross-trainer, bike and rowing machine are some examples). From a purely cardiovascular aspect, both of these types of machines can basically be used for the same effect: better heart health, improved blood circulation, etc. However, when it comes to the capacities they can be used to develop, these kinds of machines have very different effects.

Consider what happens if you begin your exercise by just standing or sitting there, doing nothing. What happens is very different on these two types of machines. If at any moment you stop while the treadmill is running, you will fall off, whereas on the static machine, you can just stop and nothing will happen. With this in mind, you can see how you can develop very different capacities by using the two different types of machines.

Stationary machines like bikes and cross-trainers are great for developing a capacity of *proactivity*, because if you don't do anything then nothing happens! You need to drive the machine with your own energy. Conversely, treadmills are very useful in building the capacity to *persevere, be resilient* and *keep going*, because if you don't keep going, then you are going to fall off! You don't need to worry about getting things started, but you do need to worry about keeping things going! Of course, you could choose to step off the belt at any time, but the choice to actually step off is very different from the choice to simply stop moving. It requires a new action, rather than just choosing to stop.

CONSCIOUS MOVEMENT

As outlined in Chapter 17, there is movement and there is *conscious movement*. By being conscious of how you move physically and focussing on your objective, you can build the capacity to embody certain key emotional and mental aspects of leadership that will support you as you move and have others choose to move with you.

Conscious movement is fundamental not only to leadership, but also to life and learning as a whole. One of the prime benefits of exercise is that it gets your blood circulating and pumping around your body. In order to live (and love), you need your blood moving around your body. When you stop moving, you stop learning and ultimately you stop living.

How do you know when someone is dead? When they stop moving!

PERSONAL REFLECTION

Marcus: Building Capacities with Exercise

I rediscovered exercise in my late 30s and for the first five years or so after that, I did not really consider the impact that my fitness work could have on my personal development in other areas, outside of the basic things that I had heard about self-confidence and endorphins, etc. Then I started working with somatic coaches, such as Chris and Beatriz at NFA, and I quickly began to connect the dots between their work and the world of exercise, fitness and nutrition. For me, this was a transformational leap and the spark that led us to write this book.

I began to see links between distinctions in exercise and distinctions in personal development to which I had previously been blind. This allowed me to shape my exercise regime not just according to what health, fitness or physical goal I wanted to achieve, but also according to the emotional and mental states I wanted to create and the capacities I wanted to develop. As I did this, some forms of exercise became more important to me, while others became less important.

As an example, what I had noticed in my personal development and leadership journey was that certain themes tended to emerge. Strength and perseverance were a strong suit for me: I am determined and keep going in the face of difficulty. I also found flexibility and creativity to be another of my strong suits: I can think around problems rather than always needing to be linear and literal.

However, I also noticed that stability and the ability to stay on *my own* purpose was often a challenge for me. This became especially evident in my current environment, where I am surrounded by a number of very strong characters, my fellow personal development trainers and coaches. I often ended up persevering and being flexible, but on *someone else's* agenda! Additionally, power and the ability to make an impact were also a challenge for me. In the face of these strong characters, I did not always make sure that my voice was being heard and that my presence was being felt (despite being 6 feet and 2 inches tall!).

With this in mind, I began to focus more on sprinting, interval and SAQ training (to develop power) and core training (to develop stability). Once I started experimenting with altering the balance of my workouts in this way, I began to notice a shift: focussing on power and stability created a marked improvement in my overall performance. The shift did not happen immediately, but it definitely made itself felt. I also noticed that not only did I need to focus on the link between the exercise and the desired effect, I also needed repetition. I have not entirely eliminated flexibility, strength and endurance training. They continue to have relevance in my journey, but they are no longer the focus of my efforts.

For me, exercise is simply a targeted form of movement. Your body is designed to move. From a physical standpoint, while being static might initially be comfortable, staying static will eventually lead to massive discomfort. This has a direct analogy with many people whom I coach. Over many years, they have been steadily reducing the movement in their lives, both physically and metaphorically; they come to me in an effort to get their bodies and their lives moving again.

Move your body, move your life!

CONSCIOUS PRACTICE

If you wish to powerfully develop your desired capacities through the Dynamic Energetic movements, then the keys are repetition (Physical State Pillar) and being conscious (Mental State Pillar) of that to which you are emotionally connected (Emotional State Pillar). Not only does your body need to experience the movements on a regular basis, but you also need to be clear and focussed on your purpose for doing these movements. In short, you need to be *conscious*.

By combining the power of your Physical and Mental State Pillars,
you can supercharge your efforts to develop the experiences of certainty, lightness,
tenacity, excitement and calmness in your Emotional State Pillar.

Remember to practise the movements with good form. If you need a reminder, do take a moment to go back to the photos of Sari demonstrating the movements with good form in Chapter 27. Remember, practising a poor habit just makes things worse and can lead to injury. Be conscious of what you practise!

In Appendix III you will find a sample training programme that brings together the seven fundamental movements, the five Dynamic Energetics and their associated capacities and experiences. Using such a training programme allows you to take advantage of fitness and body movement theory in such a way as to develop new levels of engagement and leadership. Such a holistic approach supports you in becoming physically energised, mentally focussed, and fully aligned with that to which you are emotionally connected.

29

MORE WAYS TO MOVE

There is another key element to consider with movement in the context of leadership: are you moving *towards* something or *away from* something? At first glance, it might seem to make little difference so long as you are moving in the "right" direction. However, this is another important distinction in the field of personal effectiveness, as the two distinctions tend to produce very different kinds of results. One is not *better* than the other, but they do produce different types of results.

When you are concerned with moving *away from* something, your results will tend to resemble the motions of a yo-yo. The best example of this is dieting or losing weight. If you want to get away from weighing 100 kg, then you can work hard and when you get to 95 kg, you can congratulate yourself on getting away from 100 kg and stop. However, in such a case, it is very difficult to remain at 95 kg, because that was never the goal, and there is an inevitable slide back towards 100 kg; even at 99.9 kg, you can still say you have "won" by being lighter than when you started. Then, when you hit 100 kg again, you sigh and the whole cycle repeats. This kind of "away-from" thinking tends to lead to feelings of frustration and disappointment. This is a reactive game, a process of avoiding something. The difficulty with this type of thinking is that your brain does not process negatives very well, so if you say, "I don't want to be 100 kg", then your brain just focuses on the 100 kg and you inexorably slide back towards that weight.

However, if instead you set up a goal that you want to work *towards*, such as reaching 95 kg or a specific waist or dress size, then it becomes a wholly different experience. Rather than focus on *resisting* your current size, you instead acknowledge and accept your starting point and then focus on and visualise the new result that you want to create. This time, when you reach 95 kg, you can celebrate the win, feel a sense of achievement and pride and set up a new goal, even if the new goal is to maintain that weight. This type of "towards" thinking tends to lead to feelings of excitement and progress. Now the game becomes proactive and about creation; it is a game of action, not reaction. More importantly, when it comes to personal effectiveness and leadership, "towards" thinking tends to lead to more sustainable results.

One of the biggest areas where "away-from" thinking occurs is with regard to self. For example, once I develop a belief that I am not good enough (or intelligent enough, beautiful enough, etc.), then my whole life becomes about *proving* that I *am* good enough, beautiful enough, etc. This kind of approach to life can certainly produce results, but it is a hard, lonely road paved with dissatisfaction because you never win; there is *always* someone better, cleverer, prettier, etc. out there, and that self-assessment is mighty sticky!

In contrast, "towards" thinking focusses not on your perceived deficiencies, but rather on your vision and who you want to be in the world. This is a very freeing approach, full of creativity and possibilities. This is where long-term personal development lives. You are no longer spending energy on resisting and running away from something, instead you are using your precious energy to manifest your purpose in the world, what it is that you want to lead for.

"Away-from" thinking does have its place: the classic burning platform can be a great motivator, but it tends to produce short-term bursts of energy and achievement rather than long-term shifts in performance. Whereas "away-from" thinking tends to produce an attitude of playing to avoid losing, "towards" thinking tends to produce an attitude of playing to win.[19]

CHARISMA

There is another aspect to leadership that shows up very clearly in movement: charisma. In my experience coaching middle and senior managers, the desire to be charismatic is very common. These clients all ask questions such as "How do I inspire people?", "How do I light people up?" and "How do I have people look at me and say *wow*?"

Charisma is intrinsically linked to movement. Charismatic leaders *move*; they do not just sit or stand there, motionless. Movement commands attention and serves to indicate a certain level of comfort with oneself and with the situation; it is the opposite of the "freeze" response that you experience when you are scared. It is true that the "flight" response to fear is also a kind of movement, but the movement I am referring to here is *chosen* and *conscious* movement, rather than an automatic flight response. When you experience someone as charismatic, you experience them as *certain* and free from the frozen pull of self-doubt that turns others into statues.

Charisma is generally defined as "compelling attractiveness", and human beings tend to find certainty and freedom very attractive. Movement is a major factor through which leaders communicate those two qualities. You experience someone as charismatic because you experience them as free, and people who are free *move*. They are not shackled by doubts and uncertainties. Where doubt and uncertainty lead to paralysis, certainty and freedom lead to release and mobilisation.

---

19   For more on "towards" thinking and "away-from" thinking, you can check out our friend Janis Ericson's book *I Know I Need to Change, But How?: A Guide to Taking Control of Your Life and Work*.

Moreover, the movement of charismatic leaders is not limited to movement in the domain of the Physical State Pillar. Charismatic leaders are not emotionally frozen either. They exhibit movement in their Emotional State Pillar when they are moved by events and when they move other people emotionally. They allow themselves to be moved by their purpose, and it is this emotional connection to their purpose that connects you with them. The Emotional State Pillar is a powerful connector. Similarly, they exhibit movement in their Mental State Pillar when they embrace new possibilities and new ways of thinking, rather than being stuck on one approach.

LIFE MOVES TOO

Although in this section we have been focussing on how movement relates to an individual, one other very powerful aspect to understand is that in life, the "game" itself also moves! Many clients whom we coach fail to see this, and as a result, their careers stall and their lives plateau. The ones who fail to recognise this movement end up dissatisfied, frustrated and angry, and often construct a great story to explain their situation, with reasons such as "my boss does not like me", "my team is not good enough", "my wife/husband does not support me", "I have children now", "I am too old for that now", and the story never ends. However, very often, what is really going on is that the game has moved and they have not realised it.

The Game of Business

Organisations tend to be shaped like a pyramid, with a CEO (or chairperson) at the top, middle management in the middle, and junior staff at the bottom (see Figure 29.1).

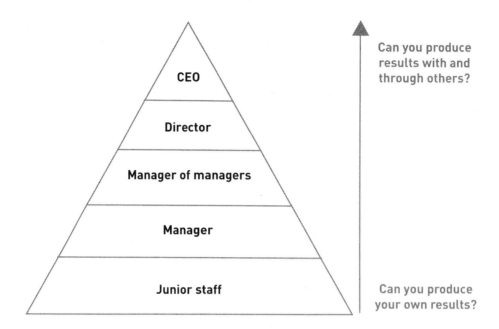

Figure 29.1 The Game of Business

When you are at the bottom of the pyramid as junior staff, the game is simple: essentially you have to prove that you know your stuff and can get your job done. If you win at this level, then you start progressing up the levels of the pyramid. It is when you reach middle management that the game begins to shift: it becomes less about proving your own worth (you have already done that); the focus is now on proving that you can have the *other people on your team* win as well. Very often, the most difficult element of this transition point is for a new manager to "let go" of their old duties, which they were very good at, and begin delegating and developing others. If you win at this level, then the next level is about being able to forge powerful relationships with people *outside your team*—your peers and stakeholders (inside and outside the company)—and produce excellent results with and through them.

The apex of this game is most obviously at the top of the pyramid. A CEO is not assessed on their ability to produce their own results. However good the CEO is at their own functional job, there is only *one* of them, and they have hundreds, sometimes thousands, of people who report directly and indirectly to them. Similarly, they have a myriad of relationship networks with which they need to work effectively. To be a great CEO, you need to be great at having other people win, producing results with and through others, as well as forging powerful peer-to-peer relationships.

The game moves substantially between junior manager level and CEO level. This sounds obvious, and yet so many people whom we work with totally miss this shift when it comes to their own career. Take a moment to consider your own career and think about whether it has plateaued anywhere or whether you are experiencing frustration in any area. If that is the case, then perhaps you are using a strategy that was effective at a previous level, but is now holding you back at your current level.

The Game of Life

It is not only the corporate game that moves. The game of life also moves, and once again, many people fail to see it because it is always easier to see something in theory than when you are in the thick of it. Figure 29.2 illustrates a typical example of the various levels in the game of life:

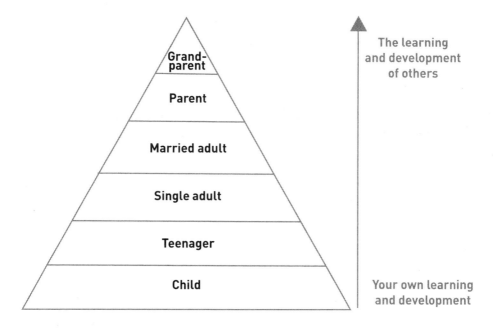

Figure 29.2 The Game of Life

The game of life as a youngster is very different from that of a teenager, which is also very different from that of a single adult. The game moves again if you get married, if you have children, if the children leave home, if you retire, if you become a grandparent, etc. Of course, your own life may or may not contain these exact levels (you may not get married or have children, for example), however, the game still moves as you age.

Frequently, we find that people love one particular level in the game and try to cling on to it for as long as possible. This generally results in increasing desperation, frustration and resentment. An example is the 40-year-old who constantly harks on about their student days and attempts to party as long, hard and often as they used to in order to prove that they have still "got it".

The game of life moves in a similar way to the game of business: as you progress, having other people win becomes more and more important. In business life, once you have proven your own ability, the game moves towards having your direct reports win, and it just gets bigger from there. Similarly, the game of life quickly moves from focussing on yourself to focussing on your partner, your children, your parents, your grandchildren, etc. Both the game of business and the game of life ultimately move towards becoming games of leadership and enrollment: having other people grow, develop and win.

If you can successfully navigate these moving games and focus on having other people win, then they are far more likely to choose to follow you. This is leadership 101, as we have outlined in Chapter 22. Consider for a moment if your life has plateaued anywhere, and if it has, then why? What level are you at, and based on your results, is your strategy still effective?

**PART III:
SELF-REFLECTION**

It is time once again for you to pick up your pen and answer some key questions. Remember, in order for this to be a valuable exercise, you need to be honest so that you know exactly what you need to work on. Only then can you create an effective strategy to improve your personal and leadership performance.

Leadership

Think about the people that you choose to follow. These can be people at work or in your personal life.

1. The people I choose to follow are:

2. I choose to follow them because:

Take a closer look at your answers above. What are the main factors behind your choice?

3. The main reasons I choose to follow someone are:

Why do you think someone would choose to follow *you*?

4. I think someone would choose to follow me because:

5. What I notice about my answer is:

Impact Intended versus Impact Felt

This can be a very challenging exercise because it requires both you and the other parties to be open and vulnerable. However, if you and they are willing to take the risk, then it can also be immensely rewarding for all concerned.

1. The impact that I *intend* to have on others is:

2. Based on the feedback I have received, the *actual* impact that I have on others is:

3. What surprised me (pleasantly or otherwise) about the feedback that I have received is:

Leader *Of* versus Leader *For*

What are you a leader for? Remember, these are qualities that you stand for or can be relied upon to bring forth.

1. Based on my *results*, I am currently a leader for:

2. I want to be a leader for:

Requests and Offers

1. I find it harder to make:
   Requests/Offers

2. I find it more uncomfortable to make requests/offers (select the appropriate word) because:

Think of the areas in your life you are currently willing and unwilling to make clear requests and offers, with whom, and the reasons why.

Requests

1. I am willing to make requests in these areas:

2. I am willing to make requests of these people:

3. I am willing to make requests of these people in these areas because:

4. I am unwilling to make requests in these areas:

5. I am unwilling to make requests of these people:

6. I am unwilling to make requests of these people in these areas because:

Offers

1. I am willing to make offers in these areas:

2. I am willing to make offers to these people:

3. I am willing to make offers to these people in these areas because:

4. I am unwilling to make offers in these areas:

5. I am unwilling to make offers to these people:

6. I am unwilling to make offers to these people in these areas because:

If you are willing to answer honestly, you will begin to see the assessments that you habitually make regarding yourself and the people around you:

- The people you hold as capable or incapable.
- Where you hold yourself as capable and incapable.
- The people you are willing to risk making a request of and the people you are unwilling to risk making a request of.
- The people you are willing to risk making an offer to and the people you are unwilling to risk making an offer to.
- The people with whom you are willing or unwilling to risk being vulnerable.
- The domains in which you are willing or unwilling to risk being vulnerable.
- The people you trust and feel trusted by.

You will also begin to notice that your experience of life and your results are very different in areas where you risk making requests and offers and areas where you do not take these risks.

Appreciation

Think about the last time you showed *sincere* appreciation.

1. The people whom I have recently appreciated are:

2. I showed my appreciation to them because:

Pay close attention to your answers. Who is on this list, and who is not? Why?

3.   What I notice about my answers is:

Resilience

1.   The areas where I see myself as full of resilience are:

2.   The areas where I see myself lacking resilience are:

This exercise can be very revealing, because it can show you where in your life you are emotionally connected to what you are doing and where the emotional connection is lacking.

Vulnerability

1. The areas of my life where I see myself as willing to be vulnerable are:

2. The areas of my life where I see myself as being unwilling to be vulnerable are:

What do you see in this mirror? What do you see that encourages you to be vulnerable? What inhibits you from being vulnerable? What do you notice about how the nature of different relationships influences your willingness to be vulnerable?

3. What I notice about my answers regarding vulnerability:

Building Capacities

Review the five capacities that we introduced with the Dynamic Energetics: Stability (to stay on purpose), Flexibility (to move with flow), Strength (to persevere), Power (to generate impact) and Restoration (to recover). Based on your ability and level of comfort in exhibiting these five capacities, rank them below. Use concrete examples to back up your ranking.

1.

2.

3.

4.

5.

Take a look back at the self-reflection exercise you completed in Chapter 27 after doing the Dynamic Energetic movements. Compare your ranking of the movements with your ranking of the five capacities above. It is very likely that there will be a marked correlation between these two lists. Which capacities do you embody effectively? Which capacities do you need to work on?

6. Based on my results, it would benefit me to develop these capacities:

"Towards" Thinking and "Away-From" Thinking

Think about where you are exhibiting these two different patterns of thinking in your life.

1. The areas where I use "towards" thinking are:

2. The areas where I use "away-from" thinking are:

Compare your physical, mental and emotional states regarding these areas of your life. It is likely that you will notice a marked difference between the two. How can you reframe "away-from" thinking goals so that they become "towards" thinking in nature?

Away-From	Reframed as	Towards

The Game of Business

Consider your own career and whether it has plateaued anywhere. If it has, then note down here where it has plateaued and how the game of your career has moved over time. Very often the plateau occurs because you are still playing the same game that helped you achieve your most recent promotion, and you have failed to notice that the game has since moved on.

1. My career has plateaued in these areas:

2. The strategy that I used in order to get promoted was:

3. At my current level of the business, the game now requires:

Take a look at your answers above. Has the game moved? Have you been keeping up with the movements of the game, or are you still playing at the previous level?

The Game of Life

Consider your life as a whole and whether it has plateaued or whether you feel stuck anywhere.

1. My life has plateaued/I feel stuck in these areas:

2. The strategies that I have successfully used in the past are:

3. Based on my current life stage, the game of life now requires me to:

Pay attention to your answers above. Has the game moved on without you? Have you been keeping up with the movements of the game, or are you still playing at the previous level?

This brings the third and final part of the journey to a close. While we have introduced P.E.R.M. as a new model to improve your leadership development, you will have noticed that we have not forgotten about the Five Pillars of Performance; they underpin this new model. The P.E.R.M. model works in an integrated manner with the three Internal Pillars of Performance. To review, each leadership fundamental relies on your Mental, Emotional and Physical State Pillars in these ways:

- A powerful **Purpose** is cognitively understood (Mental State Pillar), experienced as emotionally important (Emotional State Pillar) and put into action via the speech acts of requests and offers (Physical State Pillar).
- **Energy** is maximised when you believe you are doing the right thing (Mental State Pillar), when you feel emotionally connected to what you are doing (Emotional State Pillar) and when you have effective nutrition and embodied movement practices (Physical State Pillar).
- **Resilience** is developed through the stress and recovery system (Physical State Pillar) and is easier to sustain when you are emotionally connected to what you are doing (Emotional State Pillar) and when you believe, based on prior experience, that you can overcome the challenges involved (Mental State Pillar).
- **Movement** operates not only with regard to action (Physical State Pillar) but also in the willingness to be open to new ideas (Mental State Pillar). Finally, Movement is very often most powerfully generated and sustained by an emotional connection to your destination (Emotional State Pillar).

Taken as a whole, these four leadership fundamentals come together to create a powerful framework for improving your leadership. This is a system that has created great results not only for us but also for the people with whom we work.

You may have noticed that of the four leadership fundamentals, Movement takes up four whole chapters on its own, compared to one each for the other leadership fundamentals. This is no accident. Just as we have sought to shift the discussion onto the Physical State Pillar, we are also looking to demonstrate the powerful impact that movement, especially *conscious* movement, can have on your personal and leadership development. You can have a clearly defined purpose, sufficient energy and high resilience, but all that means nothing unless you move. It is only when you move that you can begin to create change in yourself and the people around you.

Your journey in this book may be coming to an end, but your real journey has only just begun. In the conclusion, we will take stock of how far you have come in this book, as well as how to now move forward in your journey in the world.

MOVING FORWARD

BY MARCUS & SARI

30

ENGAGING WITH THIS BOOK

We began Part I with a discussion on how human beings habitually listen to agree or disagree, using the concept of "X's" and "O's". Now that you have come to the end of the book, it is time to reflect on how you have "digested" and "listened to" what this book has to offer.

Did you just read it straight through? Did you pause, reflect and make notes where asked? If so, were you honest? Did you find an emotional connection to what you were reading? Did you ensure that you understood everything in the book, or did you just skip the parts you did not understand?

There is a lot you could learn about yourself by stopping for a moment and reflecting on how you approached this book. In particular, pay attention to any excuses and justifications that pop up ("I didn't have time to make notes", "the movements were too difficult", "the information was too complicated", etc.).

Now stop for a moment and see if you can see any parallels between the way you read this book and the way you approach life in general. For example, maybe you skimmed it all the way through, making snap judgements as you went—where else do you do that, and how is that working for you? Or maybe you were constantly picking the book up and putting it down in a disjointed and rather haphazard manner, with no real rhythm. Where else do you do that? What are the consequences of that approach? If you keep using that approach, will it create the results you say you want in your life?

In particular, think about whether you were willing to get yourself into *action* as you read the information. Were you willing to pick up your pen to do the self-reflection exercises at the end of each part? Have you incorporated the movements from Parts II and III into your life? Have you altered your nutrition habits or your exercise patterns?

Did you allow any "O's" into your box of "X's", or did you just immediately agree or disagree with everything as you went along? In short:

Were you willing to experience any discomfort in your
Physical, Mental and Emotional State Pillars as you read this book?

If your honest answer to that question is "yes", then congratulations, you are on the path to making something different happen in your life. If your honest answer to that question is "no", then congratulations, you are still on the same path of life as you were before you picked up this book.

THE CHOICE IS YOURS

The choice is yours: keep producing the same results, or make a shift and produce new and different results. It is not our job or the job of this book to tell you that you *should* do something different. All we can do is provide you with new distinctions that may allow you to see where you are in a different light, and then to illuminate a path that can take you in a particular direction. Whether you want to be on that path is entirely up to you. Ultimately, this book will "work" if it supports you to achieve your purpose in life.

Throughout the book, we have stressed that a big part of having anything work for you is to physically *move*, because *action*, rather than *reflection*, is ultimately where life, growth, learning, development, leadership and peak performance all happen. This action is a manifestation of emotionally connected relationships and conversations with others.

If you have simply engaged with this book cognitively without taking any action to alter your physical state, then we predict that nothing much is going to happen for you in the medium to long term. Involving your Physical State Pillar in your development and your journey through life is fundamental if you want to keep developing and growing in a sustainable manner.

With that in mind, if you are sincere in your desire to make something happen as a result of reading this book, then we offer you this little mantra that we use with our coaching clients: "Start *now* and start *small*." In our experience, people can be divided into two types when it comes to putting new behaviours into place.

Some people resist getting started at all. There always seems to be a reason in their Mental State Pillar or a feeling in their Emotional State Pillar not to start now: "now is not the right time", "I don't know how to do it perfectly yet", "I don't feel like it", "I worry that my boss/spouse/kids will not like it", etc. These are the great procrastinators, and underneath most, if not all, of their protestations is fear: fear of losing face, making a mistake or hurting someone's feelings—ultimately a fear of experiencing discomfort.

PERSONAL REFLECTION

Marcus: Procrastinating

I recognise the first type in myself. It took me a long time to get started on this book! Why? Because I still don't know enough and it will not be perfect if I write it now.

The critical factor that got me through this barrier was finding a purpose to which I was emotionally connected:

- Writing a book was a nice idea and I had the mental and physical energy to do it. That had been true for five years.
- Writing a book that *I could put in the hands of my fathers* was an idea to which I had an emotional connection.
- My fathers are not getting any younger. After five years of justifying, making excuses and delaying, I wrote the majority of my parts of this book in the month after I found this emotional connection to my purpose.

It was exactly the same for me when it came to getting married. I had found excuses for not marrying until I reached the age of 40. Then I met Sari and my emotional connection to her was so strong that all the rationalisations and justifications simply melted away!

In both cases, it was the emotional connection to a purpose that proved to be the catalyst which broke me free from the prison of my procrastination.

Other people have no problem whatsoever with getting started. The word that they resist in the mantra is not "now", but "small". For these people, they want to be on top of Mount Everest today. They are not interested in the small steps to get there. Their Mental State Pillar has them saying things such as: "that's too easy", "it will take too long if that's all I do", "there's no challenge in that", "what's the point?", etc. When you are attempting to lead or coach somebody like this, watch out, because they sound very committed to put things into action, and they probably are. But in reality, these people are often committed to getting *started*, rather than actually finishing!

People with this mentality tend to quickly experience discomfort in their Emotional State Pillar and become frustrated, blow up or get bored along the way. They have tried to run before they can walk, and when they inevitably fall over, they tell themselves "it is impossible for me", "it will take too long" or "something else is more important now", and they go looking for something else to start and then the cycle repeats itself!

Which do you resist the most, starting *now* or starting *small*?

31

FINAL WORDS

There is no magic. There is no one way to achieve peak performance. There is no one way to lead. There are, however, fundamentals that support you to keep growing, learning and developing as you go through life, and we have sought to outline some of them in this book.

YOUR STARTING POINT

The first fundamental is to be willing to honestly acknowledge where you are in your journey right now and the role that you played in getting yourself there. As human beings, we find this difficult, preferring instead to pretend, make excuses and explain away our results in life. This unwillingness to take responsibility handicaps your ability to make an effective journey, however smart your strategy might be.

EMOTIONAL CONNECTION TO A PURPOSE

If you are willing to be honest about where you start, then you can plot the next steps of your journey with confidence. To make success likely however, you need a destination point or purpose to which you are *emotionally*, not just mentally, connected.

THE FIVE PILLARS OF PERFORMANCE

Then, if you are willing to embrace all Five Pillars of Performance in your journey, the chances of achieving your purpose are further enhanced. Very often people are willing to embrace only four Pillars and resist the fifth one, and it is this resistance that holds them back. For example, these people are unwilling to practise effectively or ask for and accept support. Remember, while the Internal Pillars are the *generators* of peak performance, it is the External Pillars that *sustain* that performance.

In this book, we have particularly focussed on the importance of involving your Physical State Pillar and your body in development and the leadership game. This is not because the Physical State Pillar or body is the most *important* of the Five Pillars of Performance, but rather because in our experience, it is by far the most *overlooked*.

COMFORT, ENTITLEMENT AND EXERCISE

The love of comfort and the belief in an entitlement to feel comfortable are huge barriers to growth, development and performance today. Conscious physical movement, and exercise in particular, can be fantastic ways to begin to safely experience discomfort across all three Internal Pillars and to build important performance and leadership capacities, not just in the mind as a good idea, but physically as real embodied learning. As an example, you can read books and attend courses about resilience, but unless and until you are willing to put yourself in situations where you are required to *demonstrate* resilience, then resilience will only live in you as a concept (in your Mental State Pillar).

Exercise is not only a wonderful way to improve your health, it also offers you the chance to build critical leadership capacities in a sustainable manner. As we saw in Part II, a certain type of exercise (HIIT) even offers you the chance to build your intelligence and keep your brain healthy: working on your Physical State Pillar can have an immense impact on your Emotional and Mental State Pillars. In addition to fitness and exercise, nutrition also has a big part to play. If you are to continue to grow, develop and lead in a powerful manner, then you not only require health, you also require energy, real physical energy, which comes from nutrition.

P.E.R.M.

In Part III, we distilled all this down to four fundamentals of leadership: Purpose, Energy, Resilience and Movement, or P.E.R.M. These four fundamentals can all be built and sustained by paying attention to the Five Pillars of Performance.

As we have stressed many times, there is no inherent link between any of the movements, exercises or practices in this book and the corresponding capacities we have linked them to. For example, it is perfectly possible to do 100 SAQ sessions and not develop your capacity to create an experience of excitement for yourself or others.

BE PRESENT, BE CONSCIOUS

Instead, the critical underpinning factor that runs throughout this book is the capacity to stay conscious in the present moment, no matter what you are doing. If you practise remaining *conscious* of what you are doing and why you are doing it, then you have given yourself the best possible opportunity to build the capacities you want and ultimately need in order to achieve your purpose. However, today, the capacity to stay conscious in the present moment is rapidly declining. Instead, it is increasingly common for people to be physically present, but mentally and/ or emotionally absent. We even have a word for it: "presenteeism".

Consider the following description: A man is in the office working, but he is not focussed on his work. Instead, he is thinking about his wife. Then, when he gets home and gets to spend time with his wife, he is not really there; he is thinking about playing golf! When he finally gets to the golf course, guess what he is thinking about? His work! Does this sound familiar? Chances are you have been guilty of presenteeism, maybe even while reading that last paragraph!

We saw the importance of being conscious most clearly in the section on nutrition in Part II. Conscious eating is the idea of being willing to slow down and remain conscious of your eating and drinking patterns, instead of wolfing everything down at 100 miles an hour in a distracted manner. Slowing down the automatic pace of your eating, becoming aware of the physical sensations and listening to the needs of your body, rather than just listening to the tug of your emotional needs and states, is key to making effective nutritional choices. Your method of eating, like so many other routine parts of your life, becomes transparent to you because you do it so regularly, and once you lose sight of it you go onto "automatic" mode about it. Once you are on automatic and have become unconscious about your habits, you gain comfort, but you also lose your power to choose the most effective way forward.

Notice that this power to choose does not only refer to options and actions, but also to your ability to choose the *purpose* of your actions: why you are doing what you are doing. Staying conscious in the present moment, as opposed to dropping into unthinking routine, is vital if you wish to attain peak performance both personally and as a leader. This is true for all areas of your life, not just with regard to movement, exercise and nutrition.

PERSONAL REFLECTION

Marcus: Be Present, Be Conscious

When I am cleaning up the apartment, if I am on automatic mode and not thinking about what I am doing, then I can see it as a chore and it becomes very easy for me to slip into the emotional state of resentment, the physical state of tiredness and the mental state of unfairness. However, if I am conscious in the present moment, then I can *choose* my purpose: I am no longer doing a chore, I can choose instead to be supporting my marriage as a partner to my wife. Sari cooks and I clean—we are a team! It is the same action, but being conscious creates the possibility of a totally different experience.

Once I make that conscious choice, then my states are very different: resentment is replaced by joy, tiredness is replaced by energy and unfairness is replaced by equity. However, that is only possible if I stay present and conscious in the current moment and then choose.

Remember:

It is all made up!

So why not make up something empowering that will take you closer to your desired outcome?

QUESTIONS AND ANSWERS

Throughout this book, we have sought to challenge you by asking you to be honest about responsibly owning your current results and what they are telling you. At the same time, we have also provided new distinctions that you can use as you plot a new journey. Some of our approaches may seem unorthodox, but we have used them successfully with clients for many years now.

Perhaps you picked up this book looking for answers, and are now disappointed to find that instead of providing you with *answers*, we have asked you to consider many *questions*! As mentioned in Chapter 4, we believe that it is your process of consideration and your answers that matter most. Finding information and the "right" answer is pretty easy nowadays. The challenge is no longer in acquiring the knowledge, but in actually applying it effectively.

You can find answers on the internet but you cannot find your
Purpose, Energy, Resilience or Movement there.

We cannot answer the questions we pose here for you, but we hope that we have at least provoked you to take them seriously. If the book has achieved that, then we will count it as a success. If you go on from there to move and take action based on your answers to those questions, then maybe one day you too will look back and count it as a success.

We continue to develop more material all the time. If you would like to check out additional content as it becomes available, you can visit our bonus website at www.fittoleadbook.com. There you will find a blog that will be updated periodically with new articles. We will also post more Dynamic Energetic development training plans to help you develop the capacities outlined in Part III, as well as videos demonstrating some of these exercises. News regarding our Fit to Lead workshops will also be posted on this website, so make sure you check it out!

If you have any questions or feedback, or if you want to know more about our Fit to Lead workshops, please get in touch with us at **fittolead@sariusperformance.com**.

CONCLUSION: SELF-REFLECTION

START *NOW* AND START *SMALL*

Consider your response to the mantra: "Start *now* and start *small*" and where it might show up in your life.

1. I find myself more resistant towards:
    "Now"/"Small"

2. The areas of my life where this resistance is showing up are:

3. The consequences of this (for me and others) are:

Now that you see this, note down *one small thing* that you can do *in the next 24 hours* to further your personal or leadership development.

4.   One small thing I can do in the next 24 hours to get started is:

Then do it.

BIBLIOGRAPHY

Aesop. *Aesop's Fables*. Dover Publications. 1994.

Andrews, Ryan. "Body Type Eating: Find out Whether It's Right for You." *Precision Nutrition*, www.precisionnutrition.com/all-about-body-type-eating. Accessed 28 April 2017.

Berardi, John, et al. *The Essentials of Sport and Exercise Nutrition*. 3rd ed., Precision Nutrition Publishing. 2016.

Berceli, David. *Trauma Releasing Exercises*. BookSurge Publishing. 2005.

Calais-Germain, Blandine. *Anatomy Of Breathing*. Eastland Press. 2006.

Chek, Paul. *How to Eat, Move and Be Healthy!: Your Personalized 4-Step Guide to Looking and Feeling Great from the Inside Out*. C.H.E.K. Institute. 2004.

Domonell, Kristen. "Why Endorphins (and Exercise) Make You Happy." *CNN*, 13 January 2016, edition.cnn.com/2016/01/13/health/endorphins-exercise-cause-happiness. Accessed 27 April 2017.

Ericson, Janis. *I Know I Need to Change, But How?: A Guide to Taking Control of Your Life and Work*. iUniverse. 2010.

Flores, Fernando. *Conversations For Action and Collected Essays: Instilling a Culture of Commitment in Working Relationships*. Edited by Maria Flores Letelier. CreateSpace Independent Publishing Platform. 2013.

Gladwell, Malcolm. *Outliers: The Story of Success*. Little, Brown and Company. 2008.

Goleman, Daniel. *Emotional Intelligence: Why It Can Matter More Than IQ*. Bantam Books. 1995.

Lawrence, D. H. *A Modern Lover.* Blackthorn Press. 2014.

Lewis, Thomas, Fari Amini, and Richard Lannon. *A General Theory of Love.* Vintage. 2001.

National Academy of Sports Medicine. "NASM Data Collection Sheet." *NASM,* www.nasm.org/docs/default-source/PDF/nasm_par-q-(pdf-21k).pdf. Accessed 21 April 2017.

National Academy of Sports Medicine. NASM *Essentials of Personal Fitness Training.* Edited by Micheal A. Clark, Scott C. Lucett, and Brian G. Sutton. Lippincott Williams & Wilkins. 2011.

Palmer, Wendy, and Janet Crawford. *Leadership Embodiment: How the Way We Sit and Stand Can Change the Way We Think and Speak.* CreateSpace Independent Publishing Platform. 2013.

Poulos, Kelly, and Emily Liu. *Secrets to Winning.* CommonWealth Magazine. 2014.

Ratey, John J., and Eric Hagerman. *Spark: The Revolutionary New Science of Exercise and the Brain.* Little, Brown and Company. 2013.

Rigby, Rhymer, "Career Going Nowhere? Perhaps It's Because You're Fat." *The Telegraph,* 6 Jan 2015, www.telegraph.co.uk/men/thinking-man/11322225/Career-going-nowhere-Perhaps-its-because-youre-fat.html. Accessed 21 April 2017.

Rowling, J. K. *Harry Potter and the Prisoner of Azkaban.* Bloomsbury. 1999.

St. Pierre, Brian. "The Best Calorie Control Guide: Estimating Portion Size and Food Intake Just Got a Whole Lot Easier." *Precision Nutrition,* www.precisionnutrition.com/calorie-control-guide-infographic. Accessed 21 April 2017.

Strozzi-Heckler, Richard. *The Leadership Dojo: Build Your Foundation as an Exemplary Leader.* Frog. 2007.

APPENDICES

APPENDIX I:
CHOCOLATE BROWNIES AND WILLPOWER (BY MARCUS)

Sari and I are often complimented on our willpower when it comes to nutrition. However, truth be told, we are just as susceptible as the rest of the world to the lure of our emotional needs! In our own lives, although we have worked hard to distinguish the difference between the pulls of our physical, mental and emotional needs, there are still many times when our emotional needs become overwhelming and demand instant gratification. These tugs in the emotional state are very strong because they are driven by long-held happy memories and patterns of behaviour.

In particular, I am rather partial to chocolate cake, based on happy memories of my mother's baking from many years ago. However, I now have a purpose that involves eating according to my physical needs rather than simply my emotional cravings.

I have a choice: I could try and *resist* my desire for chocolate cake. In my experience, the longer I try to resist chocolate cake, the harder it gets to resist. In the end, I cave in and shovel down a big piece of sweet, sickly, sugary cake! Initially, the sensation is amazing when I give in to the temptation, but then the inevitable sinking feeling kicks in when I realise what I have done. This feeling leads me to make further ineffective promises that I will do better and resist temptation next time. The pattern is set.

However, there is another option. Instead of *resisting*, I can acknowledge and *accept* the pull of my emotional needs and do something about it. What I choose to do about it is to make my own cake, with a recipe that fits my purpose (but would no doubt horrify my mother). My culinary skills are limited to say the least, so I need a recipe that is extremely simple. Over the years I have developed one that is quick, simple and tasty, while also being aligned to my purpose. For those of you who have a similar weakness for chocolate cake, you are welcome.

Chocolate Brownies

Ingredients

Dry
1 mug of coconut or oat flour
2 scoops of vanilla-flavoured protein powder
3 tablespoons of baking cocoa (make sure there is no sugar added)
½ teaspoon of baking powder
¼ teaspoon of salt
Optional: chopped almonds or unsweetened dessicated coconut

Wet
4 fluid ounces of water (you can also use coconut water, coconut cream or unsweetened Greek yoghurt)
4 bananas
6 egg whites (I inevitably also have some yolk and a little shell!)

Preheat your oven to 350°F/176°C. Mix the dry ingredients together. Then mix your wet ingredients together in a separate bowl. Add your wet mixture to the dry mixture and blend them all together. Pour the resulting mixture into a non-stick cooking dish and bake in the oven for around 30 minutes.

The whole thing from pillar to post is done within 45 minutes. The result is one nice chunk of chocolate brownie, which has no sugar or artificial crap, with enough servings to last Sari and me for a week. More importantly, this delicious treat satisfies the strong emotional desire to have cake in our systems! Who needs willpower? Yum!

For more recipes that keep you on track with your physical *and* emotional needs, you can visit our bonus website at www.fittoleadbook.com.

APPENDIX II:
PHYSICAL ACTIVITY READINESS QUESTIONNAIRE (PAR-Q)[20]

		Yes	No
1	Has your doctor ever said that you have a heart condition and that you should only perform physical activity recommended by a doctor?		
2	Do you feel pain in your chest when you perform physical activity?		
3	In the past month, have you had chest pain when you were not performing any physical activity?		
4	Do you lose your balance because of dizziness or do you ever lose consciousness?		
5	Do you have a bone or joint problem that could be made worse by a change in your physical activity?		
6	Is your doctor currently prescribing any medication for your blood pressure or for a heart condition?		
7	Do you know of any other reason why you should not engage in physical activity?		

If you have answered "Yes" to one or more of the above questions, consult your physician before engaging in physical activity. Tell your physician which questions you answered "Yes" to. After a medical evaluation, seek advice from your physician on what type of activity is suitable for your current condition.

---

20   This was adapted from the NASM Data Collection Sheet at https://www.nasm.org/docs/default-source/PDF/nasm_par-q-(pdf-21k).pdf.

APPENDIX III:
SAMPLE DYNAMIC ENERGETICS DEVELOPMENT TRAINING PLAN (BY SARI)

This is a total body workout that will train your capacity in all five Dynamic Energetics. The purpose is to create experiences of lightness, certainty, tenacity, excitement and calmness. Adjust according to your fitness level: If the exercises feel too difficult, you can reduce the weight, repetitions or pace. If they feel too easy, challenge yourself by increasing the weight, repetitions or pace.

Instruction videos for many of these exercises, as well as other sample training plans, can be found online on our bonus website at www.fittoleadbook.com. If you haven't already done so, do take the time to answer the Physical Activity Readiness Questionnaire (PAR-Q) in Appendix II before proceeding with this workout.

WORKOUT
Total time: 60 minutes.
Equipment: Dumbbells, Weighted Ball, Cones (optional), Mat.

Dynamic Energetic	Movement	Time/Reps
Preparation	Alignment, Breathing and Core (ABC) Exercise	
Warm Up	Jogging/Skipping	5 minutes
Flexibility	Spinal Curve	1 minute
	Spinal Twist with Arm Raise	30 seconds each side
	Multi-Directional Arm Reach	1 minute
	Multi-Directional Lunge	30 seconds each side
		Controlled pace.

Dynamic Energetic	Movement	Time/Reps
Stability	Hip Raise	1 minute
	Opposite Arm and Leg Extension	30 seconds each side
	Torso Twist	1 minute
	Overhead (or Arms Extended) Squat	1 minute
		Controlled pace.
Strength (Interval Training, 2 Rounds)	Dumbbell Squat	10 reps
	Pull Ups (or Dumbbell Bent Row)	10 reps
	Rest	1 minute
	Dumbbell Deadlift (Hip Hinge)	10 reps
	Push Ups	10 reps
	Rest	1 minute
	Dumbbell Forward Lunges	10 reps (L and R count as 1 rep)
	Weighted Ball Twist	10 reps (L and R count as 1 rep)
	Rest	1 minute
	REPEAT FOR ONE MORE ROUND.	
	Rest	2 minutes
		Controlled pace.

Dynamic Energetic	Movement	Time/Reps
Power	Squat Jump	40 seconds
	Rest	20 seconds
	Rotational Weighted Ball Slam	40 seconds
	Rest	20 seconds
	Lateral Bound	40 seconds
	Rest	1 minute
	Cone Drill: Sprint, Back Pedal, Side Shuffle	3 rounds, 30 seconds rest in between. Go as fast as you can to complete each round and aim for your fastest timing! Fast pace.
Restoration	Walk around at a slow pace, taking slow breaths.	
	Front Stretch	5 slow breaths
	Back Stretch	5 slow breaths
	Side Stretch	5 slow breaths each side
	Twist Stretch	5 slow breaths each side
		Slow pace.

This workout plan incorporates the seven basic movement patterns outlined in Part II and the five Dynamic Energetics outlined in Part III. The design of the plan is dynamic and involves all three planes of motion: frontal, sagittal and transverse. The focus is not on developing muscle groups, but rather on developing high-quality movements and range of motion while developing the important leadership capacities and experiences that were outlined in Part III. In addition, all major fitness bases are covered: cardiovascular, muscular strength, endurance, flexibility and balance.

When you do this workout, pay attention to how you finish every session. It is important to finish with a reflection session. Ask yourself: What learning is occurring in your body? What will the next step be? The ability to articulate what is happening in your body is a great practice to develop if you wish to learn how to further nourish your Physical State Pillar.

Sarius Performance International is a totally new proposition in the world of Performance Coaching and Training. Formed by wife-and-husband team Sari and Marcus Marsden, Sarius Performance International brings together a variety of disciplines, including Executive Coaching, Leadership Development, Fitness Training, Sports Psychology and Nutrition, with the single-minded purpose of producing performance excellence for you and for those around you.

We call our unique coaching approach "Active Synergy Coaching" as described in our book *Fit to Lead*. The methodology involves working with the all the elements outlined in that book, including the Five Pillars of Performance, Dynamic Energetics and the P.E.R.M. leadership model.

Contact Us:

 www.sariusperformance.com
 fittolead@sariusperformance.com
 @SariusPerformance
 @SariusPerform